TASTING
PENNSYLVANIA

Favorite Recipes from the Keystone State

by **Carrie Havranek**

photography by Alison Conklin
foreword by Maria Rodale

FARCOUNTRY
PRESS

❧ For my mom, Susan, who populated my summer days with trips to pick–your–own farms, introduced me to the beauty of Amish country, and taught me how to cook and bake. And for all the tips and tricks that come out when I least expect them—I'm sure I learned them from you. ❧

ISBN: 978-1-56037-714-6

© 2019 by Carrie Havranek
Photography © 2019 by Alison Conklin

Back cover: Farmland, York County, photograph by Jon Bilous, Shutterstock.
Page ii: Harrison Wright Falls, Ricketts Glen State Park, photograph by John Bilous, Shutterstock.
Page x: The Longdon L. Miller Covered Bridge, West Finley Township, photograph by Harold Stiver, Shutterstock.

For more information about our books, write Farcountry Press, P.O. Box 5630, Helena, MT 59604; call (800) 821–3874; or visit www.farcountrypress.com.

Library of Congress Cataloging–in–Publication Data

Produced in the United States of America. Printed in China.

23 22 21 20 19   1 2 3 4 5

contents

chapter 1: Breakfast & Brunch

chapter 2: Appetizers & Snacks

chapter 3: Salads & Sides

chapter 4: Sandwiches

chapter 5: Soups & Stews

chapter 6: Beverages

chapter 7: Main Courses

chapter 8: Desserts & Sweet Treats

chapter 9: Cook's Pantry

acknowledgments

by Carrie Havranek

Cookbooks are collaborations. I owe a debt to the following:

Alison Conklin, for her natural eye for color, light, and style—your photographs exceed my expectations every time. Thanks for your unflagging good humor, flexibility, and FaceTime antics in grocery stores. You are a gem.

Thanks to Pennsylvanian Dave Joachim for my first real taste of the cookbook process with *Eating Italy*, and again with *Mastering Pasta*, and for encouraging me to join IACP (International Association of Culinary Professionals). That's where I met Maggie Green, Sara Bir, and Jamie Schler, my cookbook comrades in arms. Thanks for endless feedback and moral support. This book wouldn't exist without all of you.

Thanks to Adam Danforth for conversations pertaining to butchery. William Woys Weaver, PhD answered my Amish and PA Dutch queries; Tod Auman of Dundore & Heister gets props for his evangelical enthusiasm about sustainable butchery, along with Lee Chizmar for his generous spirit and creative approach to modern Pennsylvania food. Insights from beverage gurus Jeff Cioletti and Lew Bryson proved fruitful; Greg Heller-LaBelle helped me suss out another meadery. Troy Reynard and Josh Bushey of Two Rivers Brewing Company thought through the craft beer scene with me.

Friends near and far with Pennsylvania roots lent a helping hand. Kelly Nguyen, you are a natural recipe tester. Friends who helped me brainstorm on Facebook were great (shout-out to the Wedding Cookie Table community, Sarah Grey, Sherri Flick, and more). My Philly food pals—Joy Manning, Emily Teel, Amanda Feifer, and Marisa McClellan—along with chef Mike Joyce and Alix Griffin, were a tremendous resource. Martha Newell Maier and Berry Steiner, you know Pittsburgh so well and were willing to share.

I broke my finger in the middle of this project, and a namaste goes to Alicia Rambo for superior chopping skills, yoga talk, and good energy. Likewise, Cindie Feldman lent her skills to the carrot cake. Thanks to Pauline deKerdel Bonnet for all things French—the tartine pan, the flaky sea salt, the Espelette chile pepper.

I have big love for farmers, small business owners, food purveyors, chefs, and restaurateurs who choose Pennsylvania foods as much as possible and whose pride, curiosity, and insane—and insanely admirable—work ethic keeps them going every day to keep us all nourished.

Special thanks to my twin boys, Desmond and Miles, who many days came off the bus with big appetites to a messy kitchen and admonishments of "please don't eat that yet!" and were patient with me, and tried everything. I love you both.

foreword

by Maria Rodale

Every place has its unique tastes, flavors, and smells, rooted in the earth from which the foods are grown and traditions born, broken, and born again.

Those of us born and raised in Pennsylvania know the wood–fired scent of hams and bologna in the autumn, the aroma of roast chicken, baking apple crumbles and molasses shoofly pies in the winter, the sweet and sour taste of pickled vegetables in the summer, and the bitter tang of dandelion greens in the spring. We know these scents and flavors like we know the gentle rolling wooded hills, the vanishing farm fields, and red–brick, industrial or humble towns from whence we came.

Memories of kitchens, grandparents, mothers, and fathers standing by the stoves or harvesting foods fresh from the garden flavor our lives like salt, for those who were blessed to have cooks, gardeners, farmers, and producers counted as family.

But even if you weren't blessed with a family of cooks, if you were raised in Pennsylvania you had access to foods founded in the spirit of our industriousness and need for hard-working sustenance–whether it's a hoagie, a cheesesteak, a warm soft pretzel, or a Tastykake. Or all of the above.

Every place also has its unique tastes, flavors, and smells, rooted in the cultures of its indigenous people, its immigrants, its pioneers, settlers, and vagabonds. And as the world veers increasingly toward industrialized foods in the name of efficiency, consistency, and low cost, it's also great to see the revival in pride of place and pride in the uniqueness of our own flavors.

With *Tasting Pennsylvania*, Carrie Havranek celebrates the old, the new, and the diversity that is Pennsylvania. We are, for instance, the birthplace of Organic in America. We grow mushrooms . . . lots of them! We define chicken pot pie differently depending on where in the Keystone State we are from. We are a melting pot of hundreds

of years of immigrants from every corner of the globe. And if you weren't born or raised here, this book is an invitation to discover how Pennsylvanians of all ages are reinventing traditional foods, rediscovering old foods, and creating whole new traditions one tasty Pennsylvania meal at a time.

Ultimately food is about love. And for many of us the foods of Pennsylvania are about home. Carrie does a wonderful job of bringing the taste of love and home to anyone, anywhere. Welcome and enjoy. I know you'll love it too.

introduction

I've always been close to Pennsylvania throughout my life, but not until 2000 did I set roots here. Confession: I grew up in New Jersey, about fifteen miles from Philadelphia. I spent my high school years wandering into cafés, listening to WXPN (the public radio station for the University of Pennsylvania), and deteriorating my hearing at concerts throughout the City of Brotherly Love. But that being said, taking day trips up Route 611 with my family as a kid, along the Delaware River, took on a romantic quality; my parents had spent time in New Hope as newlyweds. I purpose-ly chose a college close to New York City, but I was tugged here for a paid internship. My first job out of college was at *Men's Health*, a Rodale publi-cation, in Emmaus. A few years later, when my then-husband and I were trying to determine whether we should live in New York City or Easton, Pennsylvania, the latter won. It wound up being an incredibly prescient decision, as the downtowns across the commonwealth are undergoing renaissances and the food scenes are lively.

So maybe circumstance is what brought me here, but I stay because it's beautiful and affordable, with access to both rural and urban elements within minutes. Pennsylvania is very much a place of opposites—large, bustling cities and tiny hamlets far from noise and traffic; stalwarts adher-ing to traditions and champions of progress. Heck, it's a swing state—both "red" and "blue," politically speaking.

The more populous cities and regions (Philadelphia, Pittsburgh, and the Lehigh Valley, in that order) offer the kind of dining you'd expect, with more than their fair share of James Beard Award–winning chefs. But acres and acres of state parks along with well-known tourism regions (Lancaster/Amish Country, Philly, Pittsburgh, Hershey Park, the Pocono Mountains, the Grand Canyon of the East, and many more) all beckon, too. Philadelphia, for example, is home to many of Pennsylvania's (and the East Coast's) best restaurants and award-winning chefs, but it's also the home of the cheesesteak, the pork sandwich, and numerous other iconic

foods that are more homey than upscale in their origins or execution—but nonetheless delicious. That one city is a microcosm of culinary experiences. Pennsylvania is a study in contrasts, and we're okay with that.

Increasingly, our old industrial centers are being reborn into mixed-use buildings with spaces repurposed for small businesses, apartments, hotels, craft breweries, distilleries, boutiques, and cafés. (Pennsylvania has an especially rich history of distilleries and breweries.) Here, we have a healthy respect for the past—many communities work diligently to preserve the old and reuse existing historical structures. But to thrive, we have to embrace the new, too. The food producers in this book are at the forefront of food right now—in some way, shape, or form, they're coloring the tapestry of sights, smells, and tastes that can be experienced in Pennsylvania, speaking to its past, present, and future.

Pennsylvania has more than 60,000 farms totaling over 7 million acres under cultivation and a keen consciousness of agriculture's importance here—it is a major industry in this state and part of its identity. Nationally, we're first in mushroom production, fourth in apple production (and Christmas trees, too!), and fifth in dairy and grape production. We have inventive farmers who are bringing back old strains of wheat. We have chefs who are working directly with farms—that often grow specific vegetables or foods for them—forging new sustainable foodways. All of the chefs whose recipes comprise this book are adding, in some significant way, their own contemporary understanding of what it means if your meal is from Pennsylvania. We have incredible farmers' markets: the Easton Farmers' Market is the oldest continuously operating market in the country, dating to 1752, and the Central Market in Lancaster is the oldest indoor market.

We are truly fortunate that we can find fresh, local, and sustainable food in most parts of the state during most months of the year, and that inventive, nourishing meals are coming out of every corner of the commonwealth, in places you might not expect. Our communities are patchworks of Italian, Irish, German, Lebanese, Polish, Mexican, and so many

other groups of people, and all of those traditions have meshed into what we eat. People care about food here. The can-do, convivial spirit of small-town America is alive and well here, and people know and care about their neighbors. Food is often key to those relationships, whether at farmers' markets, food festivals, or in the many thriving local dining scenes (college towns are particularly chockablock with fun eateries).

Thus, the happy struggle with a book like this: it's not comprehensive, nor can it be. It's a snapshot of the current state of food in Pennsylvania, with reverence and appreciation for the foods that have come to typify the state, from Amish country fare (which is far more complex and nuanced than the tourism images would have you believe) to the iconic cheesesteak, pretzels, scrapple, and pierogi. It's also a full embrace—a big bear hug—of what the chefs here are doing with the heritage-bred pork, grass-fed beef, and local dairy, fruits, veggies, and, increasingly, grains, whenever possible.

All of these reasons explain why the spotlight shone on Pennsylvania in August 2017 at the James Beard House. Lee Chizmar of Bolete in Bethlehem, along with Pennsylvania foodways scholar and cookbook author William Woys Weaver, and Tod Auman of Dundore & Heister, a whole-animal sustainable butchery, were all part of a dinner where Chizmar put a modern touch on a gamut of dishes that most wouldn't necessarily identify as "PA Dutch" or even "Pennsylvania." I was there, too, and witnessed firsthand the shock and delight of guests who couldn't fathom that all the foods they had just eaten came from Pennsylvania. I frequently make the argument, half tongue in cheek, that Pennsylvania is the California of the East Coast—minus the citrus and avocado. But in reality, that's not too far from the truth. Come and taste for yourself.

—Carrie Havranek

guidelines for recipes

Equipment

❧ Oven temperatures are listed in degrees Fahrenheit.

❧ Try to cook by the visual cues provided in the recipe or your own best judgment, rather than strictly by time. Ovens vary in their ability to retain consistent heat; so does cooking equipment. When baking, if you have any doubts about the efficacy of your oven, it's wise to invest in and use an oven thermometer.

❧ If a recipe's success is dependent on pan size, don't substitute. In many cases, however, pan sizes are adaptable—just know that cooking or baking times will likely differ from the recipe. Don't let it stop you from making the recipe.

❧ When it comes to pureeing, most chefs use a Vitamix® or other high-powered blender—for good reason. You can achieve similar results at home with a good blender, immersion (handheld stick) blender, or even a food processor, depending on the recipe. You may need to adjust how long you puree or liquid amounts a little to achieve the desired texture.

Ingredients

❧ If a recipe calls for cooking with olive oil, try to use extra virgin olive oil that has a date of harvest on the bottle and is from a reputable producer such as California Olive Ranch or Cobram Estate. Much of what passes for "olive oil" or "extra virgin olive oil" is actually adulterated. If you don't have olive oil, good substitutes when pan frying include canola or vegetable oil, or if the flavor suits the recipe, coconut oil.

❧ Flour in these recipes is all purpose and unbleached, unless specified otherwise, and measured by the dip and sweep method.

❧ All butter is unsalted, unless specified otherwise. Do not substitute margarine unless the recipe allows it.

❧ All salt is regular table salt, unless specified otherwise. Kosher salt is the preferred salt of a majority of chefs.

❧ Unless specified otherwise, sugar means granulated sugar.

❧ Fresh herbs make a huge difference. However, if you only have dried herbs on hand, or can't find something in the grocery store, remember the 3-to-1 ratio: 1 teaspoon of dried herbs can be substituted for every tablespoon (or 3 teaspoons) of fresh. Dried are more potent.

❧ Nuts are often best toasted. It's not always specified in the recipe, but it enhances their inherent nutty flavor. Toast in a single layer in a skillet over medium heat, and keep an eye on them as they can burn quickly, especially thin-skinned nuts. When they become aromatic, they're ready.

❧ A few recipes require chile peppers. The oils in some varieties can cause irritation or serious pain on exposed skin. Wear disposable kitchen gloves and avoid touching your face or eyes while handling peppers.

❧ Many recipes call for heavy cream, and substituting half-and-half or whole milk may work in some situations, but there's a reason why restaurant food tastes so good—fat enhances flavor. Just know that you can't expect the same results if you've made that kind of substitution. This is especially true when it comes to thickening a sauce, as the flavor and consistency won't be the same.

❧ Chefs love unusual ingredients—they produce surprising turns in dishes that make it fun to go out to eat. You can find many of these ingredients online. But I've also recommended specific companies in the Sources section whose quality has been vetted by either me, the chef whose dish requires it, or both of us. Experimenting with an unfamiliar ingredient is fun, and chances are you'll find another way to use any leftovers.

❧ If a recipe calls for a stock or broth that you do not have, in most cases, in a pinch you can substitute water. Of course, the taste won't be the same, but whatever you are cooking will flavor the water to some degree. I would not, however, skip making the dashi for the Pennsylvania Mushroom Ramen (see page 67 in *Soups & Stews*) in this book. The broth is everything in that dish!

Breakfast & Brunch

Stuffed Pumpkin French Toast, p. 13

Salmon

1 large (8-ounce) red beet

1 inch-long piece horseradish

1 lemon

1 lime

1 orange

½ bunch dill

1½ cups salt

1½ cups sugar

1 salmon fillet (1 to 2 pounds)

8 pretzel rolls or slices of
artisan-quality sourdough bread

Herbed cream cheese

8 ounces cream cheese, softened

2 tablespoons chopped fresh parsley

2 tablespoons chopped fresh chives

Garnish

¼ cup thinly sliced red onion

2 tablespoons capers

¼ cup celery leaves

2 tablespoons chopped dill

Serves 8

Beet-Cured Salmon

HIGH STREET ON MARKET, PHILADELPHIA
CO-OWNER AND CHEF ELI KULP

This dish has been on the menu at High Street on Market in Philadelphia since its inception in 2013. The restaurant serves the salmon on a long pretzel roll, but high-quality toasted bread works well, too. This will keep for about five days, well-wrapped, in the refrigerator.

For the salmon cure:
Peel the beet and horseradish and roughly chop, then peel the lemon, lime, and orange. Place all of these and the dill in a food processor and blend, stopping to add the salt and sugar. Lay the salmon on a wire rack on a rimmed baking sheet and cover with the cure on all sides. Refrigerate to cure for 4 days. On the fourth day, wipe off the cure and cut the salmon into thin slices.

For the cream cheese:
In a small bowl, mix the cream cheese with the parsley and chives.

To assemble:
Slice a wedge out of the top of a pretzel roll and warm both pieces. (If using bread, toast two slices.) Spread the herbed cream cheese down the center of the roll. Arrange the salmon slices on the roll and top with red onion slivers, capers, celery leaves, and dill. Serve immediately.

Crepes

¾ cup milk

1 cup flour

¼ teaspoon salt

1 teaspoon sugar

½ cup water

2 tablespoons butter, melted,
    plus more for pan

1 teaspoon vegetable oil

2 large eggs

Filling

½ cup Nutella (or peanut
    or almond butter)

4 cups mixed berries

Garnish (optional)

Powdered sugar

Whipped cream

Makes 8 to 10 crepes,
depending on pan size

Berry and Nutella Crepes

RACHEL'S CAFÉ & CREPERIE, LANCASTER
OWNER RACHEL ADAMS

Crepes aren't complicated, but they do require a little bit of finessing—if you're new to them, your first one may be a little messy. Vary the fillings as you like, but at Rachel's, one of her best sellers contains berries and Nutella.

For the crepes:
Place the milk, flour, salt, sugar, water, 2 tablespoons of melted butter, oil, and eggs in a blender and mix until smooth.

Butter a hot nonstick 8-inch pan. Ladle about ¼ cup of batter into the pan and tilt it until the batter coats the bottom evenly. Cook until the bottom of the crepe is light brown, about 2 minutes. Gently work a spatula around the edges and carefully flip it over. Cook another minute.

For the filling:
Plate the crepe and spread about 2 tablespoons of Nutella or nut butter on the warm crepe. Add the berries. Repeat with the remaining batter and filling. You can roll up the crepes or fold them in half and then in thirds, forming a neat triangle.

Sprinkle with powdered sugar and add a dollop of whipped cream, if desired.

1 tablespoon butter

6 croissants, roughly chopped

8 ounces dark chocolate,
at least 64 percent
cocoa solids, chopped

4 cups whole milk

1 vanilla bean, split and scraped

¼ cup cocoa powder

Pinch salt

1¼ cups sugar

8 eggs, lightly beaten

Serves 6

Chocolate Bread Pudding

THE CIRCULAR AT THE HOTEL HERSHEY, HERSHEY
EXECUTIVE PASTRY CHEF CHER HARRIS

This Chocolate Bread Pudding is always served on The Circular's breakfast and brunch buffets. The restaurant uses a combination of Hershey's semisweet chocolate and a dark chocolate from another of its brands, Scharffen Berger, such as its 70 percent bittersweet chocolate.

Preheat the oven to 325 degrees. Grease a 9 x 13-inch pan with 1 tablespoon of butter and arrange the croissant pieces in the pan.

Place the dark chocolate in a heat-safe large bowl. In a medium saucepan, bring the milk to a low simmer and add the vanilla and cocoa powder. Remove from the heat and pour the hot milk over the bowl of chopped chocolate. Add a pinch of salt. Stir gently to combine.

In a separate, large mixing bowl, whisk together the sugar and eggs until incorporated. Pour a little bit of the hot milk and chocolate mixture into the eggs and sugar, whisking constantly so the eggs don't curdle. Continue whisking in the rest of the hot milk until the mixture is incorporated and smooth.

Pour enough warm milk–egg mixture over the chopped croissants to just about cover them. Let soak for 15 minutes.

Place the pan inside a larger baking dish. Boil 4 to 5 cups of water and pour into the larger dish to create a water bath. Place on the middle rack in the oven and bake until the pudding is set, 35 to 40 minutes. Serve warm.

Scones

4 cups flour

⅓ cup sugar

5 teaspoons baking powder

½ cup (1 stick) butter,
    cold and diced small

¾ cup dried cranberries

⅔ cup white chocolate chips

½ cup whole milk

¼ cup orange juice

4 large eggs

Orange glaze

1 cup powdered sugar

1 teaspoon grated orange zest

2 to 3 tablespoons
    fresh orange juice

Makes 8 scones

Cranberry White Chocolate Chip Scones with Orange Glaze

A KILT AND A CUPPA, SALISBURY TOWNSHIP
CHEF AND WRITER CEALLACH TÓMAS Ó SÉ

Chef Ó Sé (anglicized to Shay) specializes in British and Irish cuisine, and scones fall squarely in that camp. Enjoy with coffee in the morning or tea in the afternoon; this one's a bit more decadent—and delicious—than the average scone.

For the scones:
Preheat the oven to 375 degrees.

In a large bowl, sift together the flour, sugar, and baking powder. Use your fingers to work in the butter until it's the size of peas; you want some visible streaks of butter in the dough. Add the cranberries and white chocolate chips.

In a small bowl, mix together the milk, orange juice, and eggs. Stir the liquids into the flour mixture until just combined. Add a little extra milk if the dough is too dry.

Remove the dough from the bowl and turn out onto a floured surface. Shape and pat into a round disc about 12 inches in diameter and ½ inch thick.

Cut the round into eight equal wedges and place on a parchment-lined baking sheet. Bake until golden brown, 14 to 16 minutes. Remove from the oven and cool on a wire rack.

For the orange glaze:
In a small bowl, mix the powdered sugar, orange zest, and orange juice. Drizzle the glaze over the scones and allow to dry until set, about 15 minutes.

Scones are best the day they are made, but these will keep, covered, for 2 to 3 days.

Roasted vegetables

2 cups cauliflower florets

2 cups Brussels sprouts,
    outer leaves removed, quartered

2 cups medium-diced
    butternut squash

2 cups crimini mushrooms, quartered

2 cups medium-diced kohlrabi

2 cups fingerling potatoes,
    washed and quartered

1 teaspoon minced fresh rosemary

1 teaspoon sage leaves, chiffonade

1 teaspoon chopped fresh thyme

2 tablespoons vegetable oil

1 teaspoon lemon juice

1 teaspoon sherry vinegar

1 teaspoon whole-grain mustard

2 teaspoons kosher salt

Freshly cracked black pepper

½ cup fresh parsley

½ cup chive spears,
    plus more for garnish

Eggs and bacon

8 pieces farm bacon

8 farm-fresh eggs

3 tablespoons distilled vinegar

1 tablespoon kosher salt

Serves 4

Fall Vegetable Hash with Soft Poached Eggs and Crispy Bacon

BOLETE RESTAURANT, BETHLEHEM
CHEF-OWNER LEE CHIZMAR

Bolete is known for cooking with as many local ingredients as possible. This iteration of a brunch staple incorporates a hearty array of fall vegetables.

For the roasted vegetables:
Preheat the oven to 375 degrees. Combine the vegetables in a large mixing bowl. Add the rosemary, sage, thyme, oil, lemon juice, sherry vinegar, mustard, salt, and pepper. Mix together, then transfer to a large baking sheet and roast for 30 minutes, stirring every 10 minutes, until the vegetables are golden brown. Remove from the oven and stir in the parsley and chives. Season with more salt and pepper if needed.

For the eggs and bacon:
Place the bacon on a rimmed baking sheet lined with aluminum foil and cook in the oven along with the veggies until golden brown and crispy, about 15 minutes.

Poach the eggs, one at a time, in a medium stockpot of gently boiling water, vinegar, and salt until the whites are set but the yolks are still runny, about 4 minutes.

To serve, place some of the vegetable hash on a plate. Use a spoon to form a nest in the hash for two poached eggs; top with two pieces of bacon and garnish with some thinly sliced chives. Repeat with the remaining hash, bacon, and eggs.

Caramel sauce

½ cup (1 stick) butter

1 cup brown sugar

¼ cup corn syrup

French toast

8 (1-inch) slices Italian bread
    or Texas toast

6 ounces marshmallow fluff (optional)

6 ounces cream cheese, softened

¾ cup pumpkin puree

6 eggs

2 cups milk (or more, depending
    on thickness of bread)

1 teaspoon cinnamon

½ teaspoon vanilla extract

½ teaspoon ground ginger

¼ teaspoon ground allspice

Serves 4

❧ *Note: You can prepare this the
night before, cover with foil, and
refrigerate. The next morning,
just place it in the preheated
oven and add another 3 to
5 minutes to the baking time.*

Stuffed Pumpkin French Toast

TRENTHOUSE INN BED AND BREAKFAST, ROCKWOOD
OWNER JULIANN BROWN

*Trenthouse is a popular Victorian inn not far from Fallingwater, Seven
Springs Resort, and Kentuck Knob southeast of Pittsburgh. Brown runs the
inn with her mom. This French toast dish is a year-round breakfast staple;
try it topped with fresh berries in the summertime.*

For the caramel sauce:
In a small saucepan, stir the butter, brown sugar, and corn syrup
together over low heat until the sugar has melted and the mixture
thickens. Pour into a 9 x 13–inch baking dish, coating the bottom
and using the back of a spoon to spread the sauce to the edges.

For the French toast:
Preheat the oven to 200 degrees. Place the bread slices directly on the
oven racks and toast for about 15 minutes to dry them out. Remove
from the oven and increase the oven temperature to 350 degrees.

In the bowl of a stand mixer fitted with the paddle attachment,
combine the fluff (if using) and cream cheese until evenly distributed.
Add the pumpkin puree and mix on medium, scraping down the
sides as needed.

Spread the filling generously on four of the bread slices. Top each
with another slice to make a sandwich and arrange them tightly in
the baking dish (it's okay if there's some space between them).

In a bowl, whisk together the eggs, milk, cinnamon, vanilla extract,
ginger, and allspice. Pour the egg mixture over and around the sand–
wiches. Cover with aluminum foil and bake 35 to 40 minutes, then
uncover and bake another 10 minutes.

Serve warm with butter and powdered sugar or syrup.

(see photograph on page 1)

1 cup baby arugula

1 (1-inch-thick) slice brioche

1 to 2 tablespoons olive oil

1 (1-ounce) slice Fontina cheese

1 large egg

1 teaspoon white truffle oil

Salt and freshly ground
        black pepper

Serves 1

Truffled Egg Toast

TRIA CAFÉ, PHILADELPHIA   ❧   OWNER JON MYEROW

Tria's stellar brunch contains this popular truffled egg toast, which looks more complicated than it really is. Timing is of the essence: make sure everything is prepped and at the ready before you get started, because it comes together quickly. The recipe serves one, but it's easily doubled or tripled, prepared in either the toaster oven or under the broiler.

Plate the arugula. Set aside.

Remove the crusts of the brioche and brush both sides of the bread lightly with olive oil. Toast the bread in the oven, 1 minute on each side, and remove promptly.

Cut the Fontina slice into three equal pieces, and then cut one of the pieces in half. Arrange the Fontina on the brioche around the perimeter, creating a square with an empty space in the middle. Return the brioche to the oven and toast for 1 minute.

Remove from the oven and place the toast in the middle of the plate with the arugula. Separate the egg yolk from the white and place the yolk (see *Note*) in the middle of the toast, directly on the bread. Drizzle the truffle oil evenly across the top and sprinkle with salt and pepper to taste. Eat immediately. Repeat as needed to feed your friends.

❧ **Note:** *When eating raw yolks, it's best to use pasteurized eggs; check the carton label. If you prefer your egg yolk cooked, separate it from the white and poach in simmering water until it reaches the desired doneness. Unused egg whites can be stored in the freezer. Keep them in ice cube trays for easy use in meringues, pavlovas, or whisked into homemade waffle batter for extra lift and crispiness.*

Appetizers & Snacks

Kluski Ślaskie (Potato Dumplings), p. 19

2½ cups flour

1 teaspoon salt

1 tablespoon brown sugar

2¼ teaspoons instant dry yeast

Scant 1 cup water, warm

¼ cup baking soda

Kosher or coarse sea salt,
   for sprinkling

4 tablespoons butter, melted

Makes 8 pretzels

Amish-Style Soft Pretzels

CARRIE HAVRANEK, THE DHARMA KITCHEN

I have such fond memories of eating buttery soft pretzels, with just the right balance of sweet and salty, at the Amish markets in South Jersey and Philly. This one comes pretty close. Pretzels are customarily eaten to bring luck in the New Year, but their appeal so transcends that tradition that it's fun to make them anytime.

Place the flour, salt, brown sugar, yeast, and warm water in the bowl of a stand mixer with the hook attachment and beat until well combined. Knead the dough, by hand or machine, until it's smooth and soft, 5 to 7 minutes. Flour the dough a little, place on a floured surface, and cover. Let rest for 30 minutes.

Preheat the oven to 475 degrees. Prepare a baking sheet with parchment or cooking spray.

Uncover the dough and divide it into eight equal pieces. Let them rest, uncovered, for another 5 minutes.

Using the palms of your hands, roll each piece into a thin rope 25 to 30 inches long. Twist each rope into a pretzel shape by lifting the ends of the rope, crossing them to make a twist, and then folding them back down on the bottom loop. Gently press the ends so they stay in place.

Boil 6 to 8 cups water in a large stockpot over high heat and add the baking soda, stirring until it's dissolved. Reduce to a simmer. Working quickly and carefully, dip each pretzel into the water and simmer for 30 seconds on each side, flipping them with a slotted spoon. They will puff up slightly in the water.

Transfer to the prepared baking sheet and sprinkle with kosher or coarse sea salt. Bake pretzels until golden brown, 8 to 10 minutes.

Remove from the oven and brush with melted butter until the butter is gone. These pretzels are best consumed while warm. They can be reheated in the oven, or frozen and defrosted later in a low oven. Top with your favorite mustard, if desired.

Shortbread

1 cup flour

¼ teaspoon kosher salt

2 tablespoons plus 1 teaspoon sugar

1 teaspoon finely chopped
    fresh parsley

1 teaspoon finely chopped fresh sage

1 teaspoon finely chopped
    fresh rosemary

1 teaspoon finely chopped
    fresh thyme

½ cup (1 stick) butter, cold

1 to 2 tablespoons water,
    room temperature

Topping

1½ cups chopped bacon

½ cup sugar

1 tablespoon butter

½ cup apple cider vinegar

1 tablespoon cornstarch

1 tablespoon water

Salt and black pepper

4 apples (such as Honeycrisp),
    peeled, cored, and sliced thinly,
    about ⅛ inch thick

1½ cups shredded
    cave-aged Cheddar

Zest of 1 lemon, for garnish

1 teaspoon each chopped
    fresh parsley, sage, rosemary,
    and thyme, for garnish

Serves 6

Apple Pie Shortbread Tart

THE MINT, BETHLEHEM
CHEF-OWNER DOMENICO LOMBARDO

This inventive sweet-savory shortbread tart is Chef Lombardo's riff on the Southern tradition of putting American cheese on hot apple pie. You can also press the pastry into individual tart shells or press them out using a round biscuit cutter.

For the shortbread:
Combine the flour, salt, sugar, and herbs in a medium bowl. Grate in the cold butter with a cheese grater and use your hands to blend until the mixture forms small pebbles. Add the water as needed until the dough becomes sticky. Turn out onto a lightly floured surface and form into a disc. Wrap in plastic wrap and chill for half an hour if using immediately. Or refrigerate overnight, then let sit at room temperature for half an hour before using.

For the topping:
In a large, nonstick sauté pan over medium heat, render the bacon; when it becomes crispy, stir in the sugar. Add the butter and cook until the mixture caramelizes, 5 to 8 minutes. Add the apple cider vinegar, bring to a brief boil, and stir until the sugar dissolves.

In a separate small bowl, combine the cornstarch and water. Add to the bacon-sugar mixture and stir until it thickens. Add the black pepper—enough to give a bit of a bite. Salt lightly; the shortbread is already salted.

Preheat the oven to 425 degrees. Roll the dough out into roughly a 9-inch circle, about ¼ inch thick. Gently press the apple slices into the dough in a fan-shaped pattern and top with the shredded cheese. Bake until the cheese fully melts and the shortbread edges are brown, 12 to 15 minutes.

Remove tart from the oven and slice into six wedges. Spoon the bacon mixture onto each shortbread wedge and garnish with lemon zest and fresh herbs.

4 sweet onions, sliced
into half moons

4 tablespoons canola
or other neutral oil

Salt and black pepper

2 pounds Italian sausage,
removed from casings

2 (10-ounce) jars pitted
kalamata olives

2 balls pizza dough

Olive oil for brushing dough

Sea salt

Makes 2 loaves

Binulata

ALISON CONKLIN, EMMAUS
TASTING PENNSYLVANIA PHOTOGRAPHER

This Sicilian celebration bread was an eagerly anticipated item at holidays in the Conklin family. The marriage of caramelized onions, sweet (or spicy) sausage, and olives is perfect. You can use the pizza dough recipe on page 97, or purchase a ball or two of dough from a supermarket.

Preheat the oven to 375 degrees.

Sauté the onions over low heat in the canola oil until they begin to caramelize, 20 to 30 minutes. Season with salt and pepper to taste.

In the same pan, sauté the sausage until it's cooked through, 5 to 6 minutes. Transfer the sausage and onions to a large bowl and let the mixture cool. Drain the olives, roughly chop, and stir them into the bowl.

Roll out the pizza dough into a rectangle and spread half the mixture onto the dough, leaving about a 1-inch margin around the edges. Roll the dough short edge to short edge, tucking in the ingredients and rolling them into the dough so they don't spill out.

Seal the ends by tucking the dough underneath itself. Brush the top with a little olive oil and sprinkle with sea salt. Bake on an ungreased cookie sheet until golden brown, 30 to 35 minutes. Be mindful not to burn the bottom of the loaf.

The bread is typically served chilled or at room temperature but can be cut and served warm once it has been out of the oven for about 30 minutes.

❧ **Note:** *You can cut the recipe in half and make one loaf, or make the full recipe and freeze a loaf for future use.*

Carrot-mushroom broth

½ cup dried porcini mushrooms

½ cup (1 stick) butter or margarine

1 quart carrot juice

Salt and black pepper

1 teaspoon lemon juice

Potato dumplings

2¼ pounds Yukon Gold potatoes

1 teaspoon salt

8½ ounces potato starch

Mushrooms

2 pounds oyster mushrooms

2 tablespoons olive oil

½ teaspoon salt

½ teaspoon black pepper

½ cup plain Greek yogurt
    or sour cream

¼ cup chopped fresh dill,
    for garnish

¼ cup chopped fresh carrot greens,
    for garnish

Serves 6 (about 42 dumplings)

Kluski Ślaskie (Potato Dumplings)

APTEKA, PITTSBURGH
CHEF-OWNERS KATE LASKY AND TOMASZ SKOWRONSKI

The specialty of Apteka is vegan Eastern European food, with a modern approach. For this dish, use vegan margarine and your favorite non-dairy yogurt if desired.

For the carrot-mushroom broth:
In a medium pot, simmer the dried mushrooms and butter for 20 minutes. Add the carrot juice, salt, pepper, and lemon juice. Simmer on low for 6 minutes and remove from heat.

For the potato dumplings:
Preheat the oven to 350 degrees. Roast the whole potatoes on a sheet pan for 45 to 60 minutes. (While the potatoes are roasting, prepare the oyster mushrooms to be roasted as well; see below.) When the potatoes are cooked through, cut them in half, scoop out the centers, and run the flesh while still hot through a fine ricer into a medium bowl. Add the salt and slowly incorporate the potato starch with your hands to form a smooth dough.

Roll a heaping tablespoon of the mixture between your palms into a ball. With your thumb, press a dimple into the center of the ball. Boil in oiled and salted water for 3 minutes; the dumplings will float to the top when cooked. Remove with a slotted spoon and set on paper towels to dry.

For the mushrooms:
In a bowl, toss the oyster mushrooms with the olive oil, salt, and pepper. Spread the mushrooms on a baking sheet and place in the 350-degree oven to roast with the potatoes for the final 10 minutes.

(continued on page 20)

To serve:
Plate dollops of yogurt or sour cream and six or seven dumplings. Top with roasted oyster mushrooms, fresh dill, and carrot greens. Pour a generous serving of carrot–mushroom broth over the plate. Serve warm with a piece of rye bread.

Peas and Bacon on Toast

VERNICK FOOD & DRINK, PHILADELPHIA
CHEF-OWNER GREG VERNICK

Chef Vernick, a James Beard Award winner, serves toasts myriad ways. This version plays up the salty-sweet balance of bacon and peas. It's addictive.

Pea butter

1 cup frozen baby peas, thawed (reserve 2 tablespoons)

2 tablespoons butter, softened

2 tablespoons cream cheese, softened

10 fresh mint leaves

½ teaspoon kosher salt

Pinch cayenne pepper

Toast

3 to 5 slices sourdough bread, cut about ½ inch thick

Sea salt

¼ cup olive oil

Reserved 2 tablespoons peas

12 slices bacon

10 fresh mint leaves, for garnish

Serves 4 to 6

For the pea butter:
Set aside 2 tablespoons of the peas. Combine the remaining peas, butter, cream cheese, mint leaves, salt, and cayenne pepper in a food processor or blender and process until smooth and creamy. You can make the pea butter a day ahead of time and refrigerate.

For the toast:
Preheat the oven to 400 degrees.

Season the bread with salt and drizzle with a little olive oil. Toast until crispy on both sides but moist in the center.

While the bread is still warm, spread on a generous amount of pea butter, covering the entire surface of the bread. Top the bread with the reserved peas and layer the sliced bacon over the toast, trimming to fit as needed.

Arrange the bread on a baking sheet and transfer to the oven. Toast just until the bacon starts to render, 10 to 15 minutes. Keep an eye on it—cooking time will vary depending on the thickness of the bacon. Remove from the oven, sprinkle with fresh mint, and cut in half or thirds, depending on the size of your slices. Serve immediately.

2 cups flour

1 packet pizza yeast

1 teaspoon sugar

¾ teaspoon salt

¾ cup water, hot
(120 to 130 degrees)

3 tablespoons olive oil,
plus more for brushing

3 ounces sliced pepperoni

4 ounces fresh mozzarella

Makes 16 (3-inch) balls

Pepperoni Balls

CARRIE HAVRANEK, THE DHARMA KITCHEN

In Erie and western Pennsylvania, this appetizer first emerged from pizza shops such as Stanganelli's. Some folks say you have to fry them, others add provolone, and still others omit cheese altogether and just bake them with pepperoni. This baked version is delicious, but if you want to fry the balls, make sure they're submerged in plenty of vegetable oil and keep a close eye on them. They fry fast!

Preheat the oven to 375 degrees.

In a large bowl, mix together the flour, yeast, sugar, and salt. Add the water and olive oil and combine for a minute or two. The dough will be soft and a little sticky. Knead until smooth and elastic, about 5 minutes.

Place the ball of dough on a floured surface and roll it out to a 16 x 16-inch rectangle. Cut into 4-inch squares. Stack a pepperoni slice, a small chunk of mozzarella, and a second pepperoni slice on each square. Fold up the corners of a square and tuck them one under the next, pressing gently to seal. Repeat on the remaining squares.

Transfer to an ungreased 9 x 13-inch baking sheet, seam side down. Brush with olive oil and bake until golden, about 15 minutes. Transfer to a wire rack to cool. Serve warm.

❧ **Note:** *This recipe doubles well to feed a crowd.*

¼ cup olive oil

½ pound sausage

¼ cup chopped onion

1 cup cooked cranberry (Roman)
   or red kidney beans

1 ½ cups Arborio or carnaroli rice

Pinch salt

4 tablespoons butter, divided

4 to 5 cups chicken stock
   or water, hot

¾ cup grated Parmigiano-
   Reggiano cheese, divided

Black pepper

¼ cup chopped fresh parsley,
   for garnish

Serves 8

Risotto with Sausage
and Cranberry Beans

OLD TIOGA FARM, STILLWATER　　✎　　CHEF-OWNER JUSTIN NAYLOR

Husband-and-wife team Justin and Dillon Naylor run a small vegetable farm and restaurant offering one seating per evening on Fridays and Saturdays. They specialize in Northern Italian cuisine, especially from the Emilia-Romagna region. Risotto is a traditional dish, typically served in the pasta or soup course—it's never a main dish. Look for imported Arborio rice, but Chef Naylor says carnaroli is even better and can be ordered online (see Sources, page 138).

Add the olive oil to a medium, deep–sided sauté pan over medium heat. Add the sausage to brown, stirring with a fork to break the sausage into small pieces.

After the sausage starts to brown, add the onions; stir to combine and cook until the onions soften. Mix in the beans, then add the rice, salt, and 2 tablespoons of the butter. Stir to combine.

Add ½ cup or so of hot broth at a time, stirring frequently but not constantly, over medium heat to avoid sticking. As the rice absorbs the liquid, add another ½ cup or so of broth. Continue this process for 20 to 25 minutes. Don't let the rice dry out so that it burns or sticks, but don't flood the rice with so much broth that it forms a loose soup.

When the risotto is al dente (not too soft, but cooked), add an additional tablespoon or two of butter and ½ cup grated Parmigiano–Reggiano cheese.

Taste and correct for salt and add freshly ground black pepper. Garnish with chopped parsley and a bit more cheese, and serve at once.

Roasted vegetables

1 pound Brussels sprouts, halved

1 pound baby carrots,
     halved lengthwise

1 pound cauliflower florets

2 tablespoons extra virgin
     organic olive oil

1 tablespoon chopped rosemary

½ teaspoon salt

¼ teaspoon black pepper

Buffalo sauce

4 tablespoons butter, melted

¼ cup butternut squash oil
     (or coconut oil)

4 tablespoons hot sauce

¼ teaspoon Worcestershire sauce

Pinch ancho chile powder

¼ cup crumbled blue cheese,
     for garnish

2 tablespoons chopped
     fresh tarragon, for garnish

Serves 4 to 6

Roasted Buffalo Vegetable Bites

THE LODGE AT WOODLOCH, HAWLEY
EXECUTIVE CHEF JOSH TOMSON

These bites combine the best of buffalo wings—but with a healthy dose of veggies. They're a best seller at the lodge, an award-winning resort tucked away in the Pocono Mountains.

For the roasted vegetables:
Preheat the oven to 425 degrees. Place all the vegetables in a medium bowl and add the olive oil, rosemary, salt, and pepper. Toss until the vegetables are well covered.

Spread the vegetables onto a parchment-lined baking sheet and bake for 15 minutes.

Lower the oven temperature to 375 degrees, stir the vegetables, and continue baking until the vegetables get a nice char and turn golden brown, another 15 minutes.

For the buffalo sauce:
While the vegetables are roasting, whisk together the butter, oil, hot sauce, Worcestershire sauce, and ancho chile powder in a medium bowl.

To assemble:
Transfer the roasted vegetable bites into a large bowl. Add the buffalo sauce and toss until well coated. Top with crumbled blue cheese and chopped tarragon before serving.

1 teaspoon olive oil

1 pound fresh spinach, washed

1 tablespoon plus ½ teaspoon
   kosher salt

8 ounces fresh leeks, chopped,
   white and light green parts only

8 ounces Fontina cheese,
   coarsely grated

1 cup finely grated Parmesan
   cheese

Pinch cayenne pepper

1 loaf sourdough bread,
   sliced ¾ inch thick

1 tablespoon olive oil,
   plus more to finish

Maldon or other coarse sea salt,
   to finish

Zest of 3 lemons, for garnish

Makes 8 toasts

Spinach and Leek Toast

VERNICK FOOD & DRINK, PHILADELPHIA
CHEF-OWNER GREG VERNICK

Who doesn't enjoy toast? It's a simple comfort food and also the perfect base for inspired flavor pairings. Chef Vernick serves this at his restaurant as an appetizer, but topped with a poached farm-fresh egg this toast also makes a tasty meal on its own. Vernick recommends Frantoia olive oil for finishing the dish (see Sources, page 138).

In a large pot on medium–high heat, add the olive oil. Add the spinach and ½ teaspoon salt and toss quickly until the spinach is wilted. Remove to a large sieve set over a bowl to cool and drain any excess liquid. Once cool, wring out excess water by squeezing the spinach into a large ball. Place the spinach in a large mixing bowl.

Add the leeks, cheeses, cayenne pepper, and 1 tablespoon salt to the bowl and mix well, making sure there are no large clumps of cheese or spinach. Allow to cool if using immediately; otherwise, store covered in a plastic container in the refrigerator for up to a few hours.

Season the slices of bread with salt and drizzle with a little olive oil. Grill or toast in a toaster so that the bread is crispy on the outside but still moist in the center. If it's a little charred, that's okay.

Spread a thick layer of the spinach mix on one face of each slice and place in a toaster oven or oven set to broil. Broil until the cheese is melted and the top begins to lightly brown—keep an eye on it, as it will brown quickly. Remove from the oven, cool slightly, and cut toast into two to three pieces. Garnish with a drizzle of high-quality olive oil, sea salt, and freshly grated lemon zest. Serve immediately.

Sungold vinaigrette

1 pint Sungold cherry tomatoes

5 garlic cloves

1 tablespoon chopped fresh thyme

1 bay leaf

Extra virgin olive oil, to cover
tomatoes

Freshly cracked black pepper
and kosher salt

2 to 5 tablespoons white
balsamic vinegar

Corn tartine

2 (1-inch-thick) slices rustic
country-style, sourdough,
or artisanal bread

2 tablespoons grass-fed butter,
divided

2 cups freshly shaved summer
sweet corn

Freshly cracked black pepper
and kosher salt

15 Sungold cherry tomatoes, halved
(room temperature)

2 tablespoons freshly minced chives

Summer Corn Tartine

MA(I)SON, LANCASTER ❧ CHEF-OWNER TAYLOR MASON

*This is what you make when the roadside stands are overflowing with corn
and tomatoes—the natural sweetness in this produce absolutely shines.
Ma(i)son serves this as a first course every summer, by popular demand.*

For the Sungold vinaigrette:
Preheat the oven to 300 degrees. Place the cherry tomatoes in a single
layer in a baking dish. Add the garlic cloves, thyme, bay leaf, and
enough olive oil to cover the tomatoes. Season with salt and pepper
to taste.

Cover with foil and gently bake until the tomatoes are cooked
through, 15 to 25 minutes. Remove from the oven and allow the
dish to cool.

Transfer the tomatoes, thyme bits, and garlic cloves to a blender;
discard the bay leaf but retain the olive oil. Blend the tomato mixture
with ⅔ cup of the olive oil from the dish and add 2 to 3 tablespoons
white balsamic vinegar. Adjust the acidity by adding more vinegar if
desired. Taste for seasoning and adjust if needed. Strain the dressing
through cheesecloth to remove any garlic ends, fibrous thyme leaves,
or solids.

For the corn tartine:
Toast the bread over a grill, under the broiler, or in a toaster until
golden brown; set aside.

Heat a small sauté pan over medium heat and add 1 tablespoon of
the butter. When the butter has melted and foamed, add the corn
and season with salt and pepper.

Briefly sauté the corn, moving it constantly, until just cooked,
1 minute at most. Remove the sauté pan from the heat, allow to cool
slightly, and then fold in the halved Sungold tomatoes, chives, and
the second tablespoon butter. Toss gently to combine, allowing the

Herbed chèvre

4 ounces fresh chèvre, softened

3 tablespoons freshly minced chives

½ teaspoon fresh lemon zest

Freshly cracked black pepper
    and kosher salt

Serves 2

residual heat from the corn to soften and warm the cherry tomatoes and gently melt the butter.

For the herbed chèvre:
In a small bowl, combine the chèvre, minced chives, lemon zest, black pepper, and salt and mix thoroughly.

To assemble:
Smear herbed chèvre onto the toasts, pile the sweet corn mix onto the cheese, and top with spoonfuls of Sungold vinaigrette. Serve warm, preferably with a chilled glass of a crispy, lean white wine.

Cheese

1 pound cream cheese,
    room temperature

1 pound sharp white Cheddar,
    shredded

1 tablespoon Worcestershire sauce

6 shakes Tabasco sauce

2 teaspoons granulated garlic

½ teaspoon cayenne pepper

1½ tablespoons dry mustard

2 teaspoons paprika

1 teaspoon salt

1 teaspoon black pepper

1 cup minced pickled peppers

Crust

1 cup chopped roasted
    Marcona almonds

½ cup dried parsley

2 teaspoons sea salt flakes

3 tablespoons Espelette pepper
    (or smoked Spanish paprika)

Makes 3 (10-ounce) balls

Whitfield Cheese Ball

WHITFIELD AT ACE HOTEL, PITTSBURGH
EXECUTIVE CHEF BETHANY ZOZULA

This is what to make for your next party—a modern take on a Western PA classic. At the Whitfield, they use housemade pickled peppers and crackers. It's hard to stop slathering this cheese spread on every available slab of bread or cracker. Well wrapped, the cheese ball will keep for several days in the fridge— if it isn't eaten first!

For the cheese:
Place the cream cheese, Cheddar, Worcestershire and Tabasco sauces, spices, and pickled peppers into the bowl of a stand mixer fitted with the paddle attachment. Blend on medium-high until the mixture is uniform and smooth. Cover and firm up in the refrigerator for about 30 minutes.

For the crust:
In the bowl of a food processor fitted with the blade, add the almonds, parsley, salt, and pepper (or paprika) and pulse until all the ingredients are evenly incorporated. Spread the crust out on a large, rimmed baking sheet.

To assemble:
Portion the cheese mixture into three balls—they should weigh about 10 ounces each—and roll each ball over the crust mixture to coat the entire surface. Refrigerate until ready to serve.

Salads & Sides

Home Fries, p. 39

Mushrooms

1 pound crimini mushrooms

1 sprig fresh thyme

1 bay leaf

2 to 3 tablespoons
    extra virgin olive oil

Salt and black pepper

Marinade

⅓ cup sherry vinegar

1 teaspoon red pepper flakes

1 teaspoon fennel pollen (*see Note*)

1 teaspoon chopped fresh thyme

2 teaspoons celery seed

1 small garlic clove, minced

1 teaspoon Dijon mustard

2 teaspoons kosher salt

½ teaspoon black pepper

1 cup extra virgin olive oil

Hazelnuts

4 ounces hazelnuts

Crispy cipollini

Canola oil, for frying

4 to 5 cipollini onions
    or ½ cup sliced shallots

½ cup cornstarch

Arugula and Mushroom Salad

MOLINARI'S RESTAURANT, BETHLEHEM
EXECUTIVE CHEF GEO DODIG

Chefs in Pennsylvania love mushrooms, which readily absorb flavors and are cultivated abundantly here. The different elements to this recipe come together easily to reveal layers of flavors. Molinari's has had this salad on its menu since it opened.

For the mushrooms:
In a medium pan, sauté the mushrooms with the thyme and bay leaf over medium heat in enough olive oil to lightly coat them. Cook until the liquid is gone, about 10 minutes. Season with salt and pepper to taste and set aside in a large bowl.

For the marinade:
In a small bowl, whisk together the sherry vinegar, red pepper flakes, fennel pollen, thyme, celery seed, minced garlic, Dijon mustard, salt, and black pepper until smooth. Slowly add the olive oil and whisk to emulsify. Pour the marinade over the mushrooms and set aside.

For the hazelnuts:
Preheat the oven to 300 degrees and toast the hazelnuts on a rimmed baking sheet until they are golden brown, 10 to 15 minutes. Remove from the oven to cool, then use a heavy, flat pan to crush the hazelnuts on the baking sheet.

For the crispy cipollini:
In a Dutch oven or other high-sided pot, heat the oil to 325 degrees. Slice the onions into ⅛-inch-thick rings using a sharp knife or mandoline, then toss the onions in cornstarch until evenly coated. Fry until light brown, 2 to 3 minutes, moving them constantly. Remove the onion rings from the oil and drain on a plate lined with paper towels. Season with salt and pepper.

Mushroom vinaigrette

¼ cup red wine vinegar

1 garlic clove, minced

1 teaspoon chopped fresh thyme

1 teaspoon chopped fresh rosemary

1 teaspoon Dijon mustard

¼ teaspoon black pepper

3 tablespoons truffle oil

1 cup extra virgin olive oil

Salad

10 ounces baby arugula

Fiore sardo or pecorino cheese,
    for grating

Serves 4 as a main course
or 8 as a side salad

☙ **Note:** *Look for fennel pollen at
farmers' markets, specialty spice
shops, and online (see* Sources*).*

For the mushroom vinaigrette:
In a small bowl, combine the vinegar, garlic, thyme, rosemary, Dijon mustard, and black pepper and whisk until combined. Slowly add the truffle and olive oil and whisk to emulsify.

To assemble the salad:
In a large bowl, toss together the arugula, crushed hazelnuts, and marinated mushrooms. Drizzle generously with the mushroom vinaigrette. Top with the crispy cipollini and finely grated cheese and serve immediately.

Beets

3 to 4 medium beets
    (1¼ to 1½ pounds)

2 tablespoons olive oil

Salt and black pepper

Balsamic strawberry vinaigrette

2 cups strawberries, divided

2 teaspoons chopped fresh thyme

½ cup balsamic vinegar

1 tablespoon Dijon mustard

½ cup extra virgin olive oil

Salad

¾ cup loosely packed fresh basil
    (small leaves are best)

1 cup cubed feta cheese

½ cup chopped pistachios

Serves 2 as a main course
or 4 as a side salad

Balsamic Strawberry Beets

REVIVAL KITCHEN, REEDSVILLE
OWNERS LIZ HOFFNER AND QUINTIN WICKS

Beets and strawberries make for an earthy and sweet combo that's popular at this small farm-to-table restaurant situated not quite halfway between Harrisburg and State College.

For the beets:
Preheat the oven to 375 degrees. Wash the beets, leaving the skin on. Place the beets in a bowl and toss with the olive oil, salt, and pepper. Roast until the beets can be easily pierced with a fork, 30 to 40 minutes (depending on how large your beets are). Cool the beets to room temperature and remove the skins by rubbing them off with a clean kitchen towel or running them under cold water in the sink. Quarter the beets and set aside.

For the balsamic strawberry vinaigrette:
Puree 1 cup of the strawberries in a blender or food processor until smooth. In a large bowl, whisk together the thyme, vinegar, and mustard. Add the strawberry puree and whisk to combine. Slowly drizzle in the olive oil and whisk until emulsified.

To assemble the salad:
Toss the beets in the bowl with the vinaigrette. Plate each salad separately, garnishing with the remaining fresh strawberries, basil, feta, and pistachios.

Vinaigrette

½ cup white wine vinegar

1 tablespoon honey

½ cup minced garlic scapes

Pinch salt

¼ teaspoon freshly ground
    black pepper

¼ cup olive oil

Salad

1 pint (2 cups) strawberries,
    destemmed and sliced

8 ounces mixed baby lettuces

1 pint (2 cups) sugar snap peas,
    cut on the bias

½ cup shaved Firefly Farms'
    Black & Blue cheese or
    any pungent blue cheese

Serves 4 as a main course
or 8 as a side salad

Field Salad with Strawberries and Sugar Snap Peas

THE BLIND PIG KITCHEN, BLOOMSBURG
CO-OWNER SARAH WALZER

This kind of fresh salad happens only once a year, when these seemingly disparate bits of produce are available. The Blind Pig Kitchen, a farm-to-table restaurant in a college town, serves this eagerly anticipated salad in season.

For the vinaigrette:
Combine the vinegar, honey, minced garlic scapes, salt, and pepper in a large bowl and whisk to combine. Slowly drizzle in the olive oil and whisk to emulsify.

For the salad:
Add the strawberries, baby lettuce, and snap peas in the bowl with the vinaigrette and gently toss. Add the blue cheese and gently toss again. Serve immediately.

½ package (about 1⅛ teaspoons) active dry yeast

¼ cup water, warm (100 to 110 degrees)

2½ cups flour

2 tablespoons sugar

½ teaspoon baking powder

½ teaspoon baking soda

½ teaspoon salt

2 tablespoons chopped fresh rosemary

2 tablespoons chopped fresh thyme

¼ cup vegetable shortening

1 cup buttermilk

1 tablespoon butter, melted

Makes about 18 biscuits

Fluffy Herb Biscuits

TALULA'S TABLE, KENNETT SQUARE
CHEF-OWNER AIMEE OLEXY

These biscuits are a snap to make and a perfect complement to any soup. Chef Olexy's "table" is situated in the middle of her gourmet shop/café and has one seating a night.

In a small bowl, dissolve the yeast in the warm water and let stand for 5 minutes.

Lightly spoon the flour into dry measuring cups and level with a knife. Combine the flour, sugar, baking powder, baking soda, salt, rosemary, and thyme in a large bowl. Cut in the shortening until the mixture resembles coarse meal. Add the yeast liquid and then the buttermilk and stir just until moist. Cover and chill for 1 hour.

Preheat the oven to 450 degrees.

Turn the dough out onto a heavily floured surface and knead lightly five times. Roll the dough to ½ inch thick and cut with a 2½–inch biscuit cutter. Place the biscuits on a greased baking sheet and freeze for 10 to 15 minutes to firm up slightly. Brush the melted butter over the biscuit tops. Bake until golden, 10 to 12 minutes.

Remove from the oven and transfer to wire racks to cool completely. The biscuits are best the day they are made but can be reheated gently or toasted for a day or two afterward.

½ loaf Italian bread,
roughly sliced

Water (enough to dampen bread;
will depend on the bread)

1½ pounds mixed ground beef,
veal, and pork

5 large garlic cloves, minced

½ cup grated Pecorino Romano
cheese

2 teaspoons salt

2 teaspoons black pepper

⅓ cup chopped fresh parsley

4 cups vegetable oil

Serves 6 to 8

Homestyle Meatballs

RALPH'S ITALIAN RESTAURANT, PHILADELPHIA
CHEF JIMMY RUBINO, JR.

Ralph's is a South Philly institution, dating to 1900, and deemed the oldest Italian restaurant in the country. It's still owned by the Rubino family.

In a bowl, soak the bread in enough water to dampen for 3 hours. Pour the bread into a colander and drain off the water, pressing the bread to get most of the water out.

In a large bowl, use your hands to thoroughly mix the soaked bread, ground meat, minced garlic, cheese, salt, pepper, and parsley.

Roll the mixture into balls a little larger than a golf ball. You should end up with twelve to fifteen meatballs.

In a large, deep sauté pan over high heat, bring the oil up to frying temperature; it's ready when a drop of water sizzles as it hits the oil. Add three to four meatballs at a time, cooking on one side for 2 to 3 minutes and then turning them to brown evenly on all sides (this should take less than 10 minutes for each batch). Transfer to a plate lined with paper towels or a brown paper bag. Repeat until all the meatballs are fried.

Serve as a side with your favorite tomato sauce, or as part of a traditional spaghetti dinner.

❧ *Note: The meatballs can be formed and refrigerated raw, covered, a day ahead of time, or formed and frozen. Defrost in the refrigerator before cooking as described.*

1 small onion, diced

2 tablespoons minced
    jalapeño pepper

¼ pound bacon

2 teaspoons mustard powder

⅓ cup dark brown sugar

¼ cup dark corn syrup

¼ cup maple syrup

⅓ cup St. Louis Barbecue Sauce
    (*see page 133 in Cook's Pantry*)

2 teaspoons Worcestershire sauce

2 teaspoons apple cider vinegar

½ teaspoon Liquid Smoke

¼ teaspoon kosher salt

¼ teaspoon coarsely ground
    black pepper

3 (15-ounce) cans great
    northern beans

Serves 6 to 8

JoBoy's Baked Beans

JOBOY'S BREW PUB, LITITZ
OWNERS JEFF AND JO HARLESS

JoBoy's started as a barbecue destination long before it expanded to its current digs, which include a brewpub. These baked beans are a favorite of whiskey writer Lew Bryson, who's also a contributor to this book. They're super tasty on their own as a side.

In a medium stockpot over medium–high heat, cook the onion, jalapeño pepper, and bacon until onions begin to turn translucent, 5 to 6 minutes.

In a large bowl, mix together the mustard powder, brown sugar, corn syrup, maple syrup, barbecue sauce, Worcestershire sauce, vinegar, Liquid Smoke, salt, and black pepper, making sure to dissolve the sugar.

Add this mixture to the stockpot, stirring well. Then add the beans and stir to combine. Simmer on low heat, uncovered, for 45 to 60 minutes (or longer, if desired). Serve hot.

Freekeh

1 cup cracked freekeh

2 cups water

Pinch salt

Vinaigrette

1 tablespoon apple cider vinegar

2 tablespoons coarse-grain
    Dijon mustard

1½ tablespoons za'atar

1 teaspoon cumin

¼ teaspoon cinnamon

2 tablespoons extra virgin olive oil

Salad

Pink sea salt

4 large carrots, sliced into ribbons

¼ cup chopped fresh parsley

4 ounces crumbled feta cheese

Serves 4 to 6

Moroccan Carrot and Freekeh Salad with Crumbled Feta

TREE RESTAURANT, THE LODGE AT WOODLOCH, HAWLEY
EXECUTIVE CHEF JOSH TOMSON AND FARMICIST DERRICK BRAUN

Nestled in the Pocono Mountains, this resort with its own organic garden and orchard is known for its healthy fare. Serve this salad for lunch or dinner—keep it in the fridge for a healthy meal you can serve at room temperature or heat up. Za'atar is a Middle Eastern spice blend that includes thyme, sesame seeds, sumac, marjoram, and oregano. If you can't find freekeh (also known as farik or fireek), you can substitute farro or bulgur.

For the freekeh:
Cook the freekeh in boiling water according to package directions until tender, 25 to 30 minutes. Transfer to a fine-mesh sieve and press out any residual liquid. Place the freekeh in a large bowl.

For the vinaigrette:
In a small bowl, whisk together the vinegar, mustard, za'atar, cumin, and cinnamon and slowly add the olive oil, whisking to emulsify.

For the salad:
Sprinkle the freekeh with sea salt and add the carrot ribbons, parsley, feta, and vinaigrette. Toss to combine. Serve immediately, or refrigerate and serve cold later.

4 cups (1 bunch) young
    dandelion greens

5 slices bacon

2 tablespoons flour

1½ cups water

3 tablespoons apple cider vinegar

3 to 5 tablespoons sugar

1 tablespoon yellow mustard

Black pepper

4 hard-boiled eggs,
    peeled and chopped

Serves 4 to 6

Pennsylvania Dutch Dandelion Salad

RODALE INC., EMMAUS
AUTHOR AND FORMER CEO, MARIA RODALE

Bitter dandelion greens, hard-boiled eggs, and salty bacon come together in this updated take on a classic Pennsylvania Dutch salad. You can forage for your own dandelion greens in the spring or buy them year-round in most supermarkets. If you use cultivated dandelion greens from the store, you may need less sugar.

Wash the dandelion leaves well, dry in a spinner or with paper towels, and set aside.

In a large skillet, cook the bacon over medium–high heat until crispy. Transfer the bacon to paper towels to drain and set aside. Pour off all but half the pan drippings.

In a small bowl, whisk together the flour, water, vinegar, sugar (to taste), mustard, and pepper. Add the mixture to the reserved drippings in the skillet and cook over medium heat until thickened, 1 to 2 minutes.

Transfer the dandelion leaves to a large bowl or platter, pour the hot dressing onto the leaves, and toss to combine.

Crumble the bacon over the salad, top with the chopped eggs, and serve immediately.

Chicken

2 chicken breasts
   (about 8 ounces total)

Salt and black pepper

2 tablespoons canola
   or grape seed oil

Salad

2 cups iceberg lettuce

2 cups mesclun or mixed greens

1 cup halved cherry tomatoes

1 cup sliced and halved cucumbers

¼ cup red onion, sliced into
   half moons

½ cup shredded soft cheese such as
   Cheddar or Monterey Jack

Dressing

½ cup buttermilk

3 tablespoons sour cream

¼ cup mayonnaise

1 tablespoon chopped fresh chives,
   tarragon, dill, or parsley

½ teaspoon Dijon mustard

1 small garlic clove, minced

Salt and pepper

Serves 2 as a main course
or 4 as a side salad

Pittsburgh Salad
with Grilled Chicken

CARRIE HAVRANEK, THE DHARMA KITCHEN

There's a curious (but delicious) custom in western Pennsylvania that involves putting french fries in salad. Its origin is attributed to Jerry's Curb Service in the 1960s, as a "steak salad." Use steak or chicken, and take a shortcut by using good-quality frozen french fries. Don't skip the homemade ranch, though; the taste is far superior.

For the chicken:
Season the chicken with salt and pepper and cook in a skillet (or on the grill) with a little bit of oil over medium heat. Flip the chicken breasts after 4 to 5 minutes and continue cooking until no longer pink in the middle. Set aside.

While the chicken is cooking, prepare the french fries according to the package directions.

For the salad:
In a large bowl, add the iceberg lettuce, mesclun greens, cherry tomatoes, cucumbers, and red onions and toss to combine. Layer shredded cheese over the top.

For the dressing:
In a small bowl, whisk together the buttermilk, sour cream, mayonnaise, herbs, mustard, and minced garlic until thoroughly combined. Add salt and pepper to taste.

To assemble:
Add the chicken to the large bowl with the greens, vegetables, and cheese. Scatter the french fries over everything and drizzle the dressing on top. Serve immediately.

1 tablespoon toasted sesame oil

1 cup balsamic vinegar

½ cup brown sugar

1 head red cabbage, shredded

Serves 6 to 8

Red Cabbage Slaw

VOODOO BREWERY, MEADVILLE
CULINARY DIRECTOR ANTHONY GLASGOW

This simple but tasty slaw is a great addition to top the Black Bean Burger (see page 51 in Sandwiches) or delicious eaten on its own.

In a large bowl, combine the oil, vinegar, and brown sugar. Mix until the brown sugar has dissolved. Add the shredded cabbage and toss. Serve at room temperature or chilled. Properly covered, it will keep in the refrigerator for up to 10 days.

Brussels sprouts

2 pounds Brussels sprouts

1 tablespoon olive oil

Tehina sauce

1 head garlic

¾ cup lemon juice

1½ teaspoons kosher salt, divided

2 generous cups tehina

½ teaspoon ground cumin

1½ cups ice water

Brussels sprouts baba ganoush

½ cup hazelnuts

Roasted Brussels sprouts leaves

2 generous cups tehina sauce

2 tablespoons olive oil

1 tablespoon lemon juice

Anchovy vinaigrette

7 ounces anchovy fillets

1 quarter red onion

2 tablespoons red wine vinegar

¼ cup extra virgin olive oil

Pinch salt

Zahav Brussels Sprouts

ZAHAV, PHILADELPHIA
CHEF-OWNER MICHAEL SOLOMONOV

*Solomonov, an Israeli-born but Pennsylvania-raised chef, regularly rein-
vents this dish, which wastes no part of a Brussels sprout. Look for sprouts
that are large and firm—they hold up best when pan fried. Solomonov
exclusively uses tahini (known as tehina in Israel) from Soom Foods,
a women-run Philadelphia business (see Sources, page 138).*

For the Brussels sprouts:
Preheat the oven to 350 degrees. Cut the stems off the sprouts and
remove the darker outer leaves. In a medium bowl, toss the stems
and leaves with the olive oil. Transfer to a baking sheet and roast
until soft, about 20 minutes, checking the leaves and removing them
if they begin to burn before the stems are done.

Slice the sprouts in half and set aside.

For the tehina sauce:
Break up the head of garlic with your hands, letting the unpeeled
cloves fall into a blender. Add the lemon juice and ½ teaspoon of the
salt. Blend on high for a few seconds until you have a coarse puree.
Let the mixture stand for 10 minutes to let the garlic mellow.

Pour the mixture through a fine-mesh strainer set over a large mixing
bowl, pressing on the solids to extract as much liquid as possible.
Discard the solids. Add the tehina to the strained lemon–garlic juice
in the bowl, along with the cumin and remaining 1 teaspoon salt.

Whisk the mixture together until smooth (or use a food processor),
adding ice water, a few tablespoons at a time, to thin it out. The sauce

(continued on page 48)

½ cup chopped hazelnuts,
for garnish

Serves 4

will lighten in color as you whisk. When the tehina seizes up or tightens, keep adding ice water, bit by bit (about 1½ cups total), whisking energetically until you have a smooth, creamy, thick sauce.

Taste and add up to 1½ teaspoons more salt and extra cumin if you like. If you're not using the sauce immediately, whisk in a few tablespoons of ice water to loosen it further before refrigerating. The tehina sauce will keep a week in the refrigerator or up to a month in the freezer.

For the brussels sprouts baba ganoush:
Blanch the hazelnuts in boiling water until soft, about 3 minutes. Set aside.

In a food processor, blend the roasted Brussels sprouts leaves and stems, blanched hazelnuts, and tehina sauce with the olive oil and lemon juice. Add salt to taste.

For the anchovy vinaigrette:
Puree the anchovies and red onion with the red wine vinegar in a food processor or high-speed blender. Whisk in the olive oil. Season with salt to taste.

To assemble:
Pan fry the Brussels sprout halves until golden brown, transfer to a bowl, add the anchovy vinaigrette, and toss to coat. Ladle a generous spoonful of the baba ganoush on four individual plates, top with the Brussels sprout halves, and finish with a sprinkling of chopped hazelnuts. Serve immediately.

Sandwiches

Barrel 21 Burger, p. 50

Maple cipollini onions

1 pound cipollini onions, halved

2 teaspoons kosher salt

3 teaspoons black pepper

¼ cup vegetable oil

½ cup maple syrup

Burgers

2 pounds grass-fed ground beef

Kosher salt and black pepper

8 strips bacon

8 ounces smoked Cheddar

4 eggs

2 tablespoons butter, melted

4 brioche buns

4 gherkins

1½ pounds steak fries

Serves 4

Barrel 21 Burger

BARREL 21 DISTILLERY & DINING, STATE COLLEGE
OWNERS CHARLE SCHNABLE AND ROGER GARTHWAITE

Finding the best grass-fed beef makes a big difference here—Barrel 21 sources locally for its restaurant. The maple cipollini onions add a layer of unexpected sweetness that complements the burger's other flavors well.

For the maple cipollini onions:
Toss the onions in salt and pepper. Add the oil to a pan over medium heat and cook the onions on each side until golden brown, about 5 minutes. Add the maple syrup and reduce until it evaporates.

For the burgers:
Divide the beef into four (8-ounce) patties and season liberally with salt and pepper. Grill to the doneness of your liking.

Cook the bacon in a cast-iron pan or grill pan over medium-high heat until crispy. Remove the bacon and drain on a paper towel on a plate. While the bacon is cooking, bake the steak fries according to package directions. Slice the Cheddar cheese for four burgers.

To assemble:
Place the grilled burgers in the pan used to fry the bacon and top each with onions, two strips bacon, and cheese slices. Cover and steam briefly until the cheese begins to melt. In a separate pan, fry the eggs sunny-side up or over easy and set aside.

Split and butter the buns and toast them on the grill, watching closely to avoid burning. Plate a bun, transfer a burger to the bottom half of the bun, and top with a fried egg and the top half of the bun. Pierce a gherkin with a wooden skewer and plant it through the center of the bun. Repeat with the remaining buns and burgers. Serve with steak fries.

(see photograph on page 49)

Black Bean Burger

VOODOO BREWERY, MEADVILLE
CULINARY DIRECTOR ANTHONY GLASGOW

Voodoo Brewery operates several brewpubs in the northwest part of the state. The menu changes regularly, but this vividly colored beet and black bean burger is a beloved fixture. You can make the filling a day ahead as long as you keep it covered in the refrigerator.

1 bunch (about 1½ pounds) red beets

2 (15.5-ounce) cans black beans, rinsed and drained

1 medium red onion, diced small

½ cup cooked black rice

½ cup masa flour

1 tablespoon smoked paprika

1 teaspoon cumin

½ teaspoon coriander

½ teaspoon dried thyme

½ teaspoon red pepper flakes

2 tablespoons brown mustard

Kosher salt and freshly cracked black pepper

2 to 3 tablespoons canola or grape seed oil

8 buns

8 leaves lettuce of your choice

1 large tomato, cut into 8 slices

Mayonnaise

Serves 8

Preheat the oven to 375 degrees.

Trim the beets, wrap individually in aluminum foil, and roast until fork tender, about 30 minutes—longer if the beets are large. Remove from the oven and let cool. Once they are cool enough to handle, remove the skins with a paper towel or by working the skins off with your hands under cold running water. Pat the beets dry and quarter with a sharp knife.

Place the beets and black beans in a food processor or blender and pulse until the mixture is smooth.

In a medium mixing bowl, combine the beet–bean mixture with the chopped onion, cooked rice, and masa. Stir until evenly mixed. Add the paprika, cumin, coriander, thyme, red pepper flakes, mustard, and salt and pepper to taste. Mix thoroughly and add more masa, a little at a time, if needed, for firmness. Form into eight burgers and store, covered with plastic wrap or foil, in the refrigerator for 1 hour or up to overnight.

To prepare, heat the oil in a medium skillet over medium heat. Cook the burgers 2 to 3 minutes on each side, keeping a watchful eye as they will burn quickly if the oil is too hot or they're left unattended. Place them on buns and top with lettuce, tomato, and mayonnaise. Serve with Voodoo's Red Cabbage Slaw (see page 46 *Salads & Sides*).

1 boneless pork butt/shoulder
(5 to 6 pounds)

2 tablespoons kosher salt

2 tablespoons freshly cracked
black pepper

2 tablespoons chili powder

1½ pounds Spanish onions,
roughly chopped

20 garlic cloves

1 bunch parsley

8 cups Iron Hill Vienna red lager

4 cups chicken stock

12 potato or Kaiser rolls

Serves 10 to 12

Braised Pulled Pork Sandwich

IRON HILL BREWERY, PHILADELPHIA
CO-FOUNDER AND DIRECTOR OF CULINARY OPERATIONS KEVIN DAVIES

*At Iron Hill, they gently braise pulled pork in beer for several hours in
the oven to make it buttery smooth, with a hint of bitterness from the beer.
Of course, the brewery uses its own Vienna red lager, but good substitutes
include Grist House's Camp Slap Red, Hitchhiker's Venn Diagram, or
Abjuration's Irish Red Ale.*

Preheat the oven to 400 degrees. Season the pork with salt and
pepper, then rub the chili powder into the meat.

Place the pork in a roasting pan and top with the onions, garlic,
and parsley. Pour the beer and chicken stock into the pan around
the pork; it should come about halfway up the sides.

Place a sheet of wax paper over the pan and then seal the pan with
aluminum foil or a lid. Cook until the pork reaches an internal temperature of at least 195 degrees, about 3½ hours. Cook to just past
doneness—the pork should shred easily with a fork.

Carefully transfer the pork from the liquid to a cutting board. Scrape
off all the cooked vegetables. Save the cooking liquid but remove any
fat as it separates. Shred the pork and place into a large bowl. Cover
the pork with about 2 cups of the cooking liquid and stir to combine.

To serve, pile up a generous amount of pork on each roll and garnish
with your favorite pickled vegetables and one of Iron Hill's barbecue
sauces (see page 133 in *Cook's Pantry*).

Cashew Chicken Salad Sandwich

THE KIND CAFÉ, SELINSGROVE
OWNER DAVIDE DELLA PIETRA

Diners at this sweet neighborhood spot can expect all kinds of homemade and nourishing soups, sandwiches, and salads. This sandwich is particularly popular and is a fixture on the chalkboard menu.

2 tablespoons olive oil

1 pound chicken breasts, trimmed

Salt and black pepper

2 small Granny Smith apples, quartered (about 1 cup)

2 celery stalks

1 cup roasted cashews

¾ cup raisins

⅔ cup mayonnaise

⅔ cup plain Greek yogurt

12 slices Texas toast bread

2 cups mixed spring greens

½ cup extra virgin olive oil, for drizzling

Serves 6

Heat the olive oil in a skillet over medium heat. Sprinkle salt and pepper over both sides of the chicken breasts and cook for 10 to 12 minutes, turning them over at the halfway point. Remove and let cool. Once the chicken is cool enough to handle, chop into bite-sized pieces.

In the bowl of a food processor fitted with the blade, coarsely chop the apples, celery, and cashews.

In a separate large mixing bowl, mix together the raisins, mayonnaise, and yogurt. Add the chopped apples, celery, and cashews, then the chicken pieces, and stir until well combined.

Toast the slices of Texas toast, then scoop chicken salad onto a slice of toast. Top with a layer of mixed spring greens and then close the sandwich with another slice of toast. Cut diagonally and drizzle the top of the sandwich with extra virgin olive oil. Repeat for each sandwich. Any unused chicken salad will keep, covered, in the refrigerator for up to 5 days.

¼ cup extra virgin olive oil,
    plus more to drizzle

1 garlic clove, minced

1 red bell pepper, sliced into strips

1 (8-inch) hoagie roll, preferably
    Amoroso's

¼ pound thinly sliced
    (about 4 slices) sharp aged
    provolone cheese

½ to ¾ pound thinly
    sliced turkey breast

Handful of shredded lettuce

½ tomato, thinly sliced

½ white onion, thinly sliced

Salt, black pepper, and dried
    oregano, for seasoning

Makes 1 big sandwich

Knuckle Sandwich

FORKSVILLE GENERAL STORE & RESTAURANT, FORKSVILLE
OWNERS MARY ANN AND "BIG MIKE" STASIUNAS

Tucked away in the Endless Mountains next to a covered bridge over Loyalsock Creek, the historic Forksville General Store is unassuming. Owner "Big Mike" is a native Philadelphian and knows how to make cheesesteaks and hoagies. This one relies on the pungency of aged provolone—when used sparingly but effectively, it packs a punch. "This one is sure to get you 'forked up' on good food!" he says.

In a medium sauté pan, heat the olive oil over low heat. Add the minced garlic and sauté until fragrant, about 1 minute. Add the bell pepper and cook until soft, 4 to 5 minutes. Remove from heat.

Preheat the oven to 350 degrees. Cut open (but not through) the hoagie roll and spread a light amount of olive oil on the interior of the roll. Place the sharp provolone on the roll and add the thinly sliced turkey breast. Layer the red peppers on top of the turkey breast.

Place the open sandwich into the oven and bake until the roll is golden brown and cheese has begun to melt, 5 to 10 minutes.

Remove the heated hoagie and add lettuce and slices of tomato and onion, then garnish with a little more olive oil, salt, pepper, and oregano. Serve immediately.

Mona Lisa

PICASSO'S, ERIE
CHEF-OWNERS DONNY WISNIEWSKI AND RAY STOLZ

Named for the esteemed, most famous painting of all time, the Mona Lisa is Picasso's signature sandwich. Picasso's cooks the sandwich for 2 minutes and 30 seconds at 425 degrees on a panini press. If you don't have one, the best way to duplicate this is to grill it in a cast-iron pan, with another heavy pan placed on top of the sandwich. If you can't find Havarti at the deli counter, feel free to substitute Cheddar or Jack cheese.

4 tablespoons mayonnaise

1 tablespoon basil pesto

1 to 2 tablespoons butter, softened

4 thick slices multigrain sandwich bread

8 ounces sliced deli turkey

1 cup diced artichoke hearts

1 cup baby spinach

4 large slices tomato

4 slices Havarti cheese

Makes 2 sandwiches

In a small bowl, combine the mayonnaise and pesto with a spoon.

Heat a cast-iron skillet over medium-high heat. Spread the butter thinly on one side of two pieces of bread. Place one slice of bread, buttered side down, on the pan. Add half the turkey, ½ cup of diced artichoke hearts, and about ½ cup of baby spinach. Spread two tomato slices so they cover the whole sandwich. Add the pesto mayo on top of the tomato, followed by two slices of cheese, and then the top slice of bread.

Cook over medium-high heat for a couple of minutes, watching carefully to avoid burning the bread. With a spatula, gently lift the sandwich edge for a peek. When it's golden brown, carefully flip the sandwich to cook the other side. Grill for another minute or so. Transfer to a plate and repeat the steps for the second sandwich. Savor your sandwiches—with a smile—while they're still warm.

⅓ cup chopped white onion

1 tablespoon vegetable oil

12 ounces rib eye or sirloin, sliced

1 (12-inch) Liscio's roll

3 slices white American cheese

Makes 1 sandwich

Philly Cheesesteak

JOE'S STEAKS + SODA SHOP, PHILADELPHIA
OWNER JOE GROH

Since 1949, Joe's Steaks + Soda Shop hasn't changed its cheesesteak recipe. For decades, Joe's been sourcing rolls from Liscio's, an Italian bakery in South Jersey, but any sturdy long roll will do here.

Heat a large griddle or nonstick pan over medium heat. Add the onions and a few drops of water. Use a spatula to move the onions around so they cook evenly without scorching.

Move the onions to one side of the griddle, add the oil, and place the sliced steak onto the oil. Once the steak starts to sizzle and brown, flip it and move it around so it doesn't burn.

When the steak is almost cooked, line it up in the pan in a pile the same length as your roll and layer the cheese on top. Pour a bit of oil on the cheese to help it melt. When the cheese is sufficiently melted, use a long spatula to scoop up the steak and cheese as a unit and carefully place it on the roll. Add the fried onions. Serve immediately.

Soups & Stews

Carrot Soup with Brown Butter, Pecans, and Crème Fraîche, p. 61

8 ounces bacon, chopped

8 ounces ground beef

1 pound ground pork

1 large white onion, chopped

Salt and pepper

1 red bell pepper, chopped

1 green bell pepper, chopped

1 tablespoon canned chipotle
    peppers

1 long hot pepper, chopped

2 tablespoons chili powder

1 tablespoon ground cumin

2 teaspoons ground coriander

2 teaspoons smoked paprika

1 teaspoon cayenne pepper

½ teaspoon cinnamon

2 teaspoons ground coffee

2 tablespoons brown sugar

2 tablespoons tomato paste

½ cup black beans, canned

1 (15-ounce) can red kidney beans,
    drained and rinsed

8 ounces dark beer,
    preferably a stout

1 (15-ounce) can plum tomatoes,
    mashed with hands

Award-Winning Chili

TWO RIVERS BREWING COMPANY, EASTON
EXECUTIVE CHEF JEREMY BIALKER

This chili is no joke: it has repeatedly won awards at chili contests. Don't be intimidated by the ingredients list—you probably have most of these on hand.

Heat a large stockpot until it faintly smokes. Trim 2 tablespoons of fat off the bacon and let it melt in the pot. Add the chopped bacon and cook for 5 minutes. Add the ground beef and pork and brown until no longer pink. Remove the meat from the pot and reserve.

Drain all but about 2 tablespoons fat from the pot. Add the onion and the salt and pepper to taste. Cook for 5 minutes, then add the red and green bell peppers, chipotle peppers, and hot pepper. Cook until slightly softened, 5 to 6 minutes. Add the chili powder, cumin, coriander, paprika, cayenne pepper, cinnamon, and ground coffee and cook about 5 minutes to let the spices bloom in the fat. Add brown sugar and tomato paste and cook for another 5 minutes. Add the reserved meats back in, along with the black and kidney beans. Cook for 10 minutes, stirring frequently.

Add the beer and tomatoes and simmer until incorporated. Add the stock, chocolate chips, molasses, vinegar, and hot sauce. Let simmer for 30 minutes. Adjust the seasoning if desired. The chili should be spicy yet sweet, with a hint of smoke.

6 cups beef or pork stock

¼ cup chocolate chips

¼ cup molasses

¼ cup red wine vinegar

¼ cup hot sauce

Serves 10

2 to 3 pounds of bones

2 carrots, unpeeled and
    cut into chunks

½ onion

2 to 3 garlic cloves

2 tablespoons peppercorns

8 cups water

2 tablespoons apple cider vinegar

Makes about 8 cups

Bone Broth

BREAKAWAY FARMS, MOUNT JOY
OWNER NATE THOMAS

Breakaway Farms, nestled in the Lancaster County countryside, is known for its grass-fed, pastured-raised beef, pork, and chicken—its slogan is "beyond organic." Owner Nate Thomas makes this bone broth frequently for his farmers and his family, and it will sustain you through the cold winter months. Use whatever bones you have—you can even "mix species" as he says, by using any combination of pork, chicken, and beef.

Fill a large stockpot with the bones. Add the carrots, half an onion (skins and all), garlic cloves, and peppercorns. Add the water and apple cider vinegar. Bring to a boil and reduce to a low simmer with the lid slightly askew. Simmer for 6 hours or up to 24 hours, skimming the foam off the top as necessary. Add water if needed—the bones and veggies should remain submerged.

If you don't want to bother with the hands-on process of using the stovetop, place all the ingredients in a slow cooker and cook on low for the same amount of time.

Strain out the solids using a fine-mesh sieve, let the broth cool a bit, and transfer to the refrigerator (in the pot) to cool overnight. Reheat again, strain, and transfer to lidded containers to cool. Remove any solidified fat from the surface of the broth. Refrigerate and use within 3 to 4 days. Bone broth can be frozen for up to a year, if desired.

1 pound carrots

4 tablespoons butter, divided

1 medium yellow onion, minced

2 sprigs fresh thyme

1 red jalapeño, minced

2 tablespoons ground sesame seeds
(pulse in food processor
or spice grinder)

4 cups chicken stock

Kosher salt

½ cup plus 2 tablespoons
crème fraîche

¼ cup crushed pecans

1 tablespoon sherry vinegar

2 tablespoons chopped
carrot greens

Pennsylvania maple syrup, to finish

Serves 4 to 6

Note: If you can't find crème fraîche, substitute sour cream or plain Greek yogurt, but know that it won't integrate as smoothly. If you can't find a red jalapeño, use a small cherry pepper.

Carrot Soup with Brown Butter, Pecans, and Crème Fraîche

TALULA'S TABLE, KENNETT SQUARE
CHEF-OWNER AIMEE OLEXY

It can be challenging to snag a spot at Talula's Table—chef Aimee Olexy changes the menu every day for her once-a-day seating and fans make reservations a year in advance. Locals shop at her gourmet market for delicious sandwiches, soups, salads, and scones, along with homemade dips and dressings and other specialty artisan products. Olexy makes this soup every spring.

Peel the carrots and cut 1 carrot into very thin coins (about ½ cup). Cut the rest of the carrots into ½-inch pieces (about 2 cups).

Melt 2 tablespoons of the butter in a medium saucepan over medium heat. Add the onion and cook, stirring occasionally, until soft, 8 to 10 minutes. Add the thyme sprigs, jalapeño, sesame seeds, and the ½-inch-cut carrots. Cook for 10 minutes, stirring occasionally. Add the chicken stock and kosher salt to taste. Bring to a boil, reduce the heat, and simmer until the carrots are very tender, about 15 minutes. Remove from heat and remove the thyme sprigs.

Puree the carrot mixture in a blender, working in batches if needed. Return the soup to the pot and stir in ½ cup of crème fraîche. Adjust the seasoning with salt, and cover the pot.

Melt the remaining 2 tablespoons of butter in a small sauté pan over medium-high heat and cook until the solids begin to brown. Add the pecans, tossing to coat them, for about a minute, until they look toasted. Remove from heat and add the vinegar.

Serve the soup in bowls. Dollop each serving with the remaining crème fraîche and the pecan brown butter, and sprinkle with the chopped carrot greens and carrot coins. Finish with a drizzle of maple syrup.

(see photograph on page 57)

¾ cup (1½ sticks) butter

2 cups minced onions

1 cup finely diced carrots

1 stick celery, finely diced

¼ cup flour

2 teaspoons chopped fresh parsley

1 teaspoon seafood seasoning
   (such as Old Bay®)

¼ teaspoon celery salt

⅛ teaspoon white pepper

4 cups milk, gently heated

3 tablespoons Madeira wine

½ pound lump crabmeat

Salt

Serves 4 to 6

Cooper's Maryland Crab Bisque

COOPER'S SEAFOOD HOUSE, SCRANTON
OWNER PAUL COOPER

If you've watched the television show The Office, *perhaps you'll recognize the name of this restaurant—or its kitschy, larger-than-life interior. Cooper's is a landmark, and this signature recipe was published decades ago in* Bon Appétit. *It's a classic.*

In a medium saucepan, melt the butter over medium-high heat. Add the onions, carrots, and celery and sauté until soft, 3 to 4 minutes. Reduce the heat to medium and add the flour, whisking until smooth. Cook for 5 minutes, whisking frequently.

Stir in the parsley, seafood seasoning, celery salt, and white pepper. Gradually add the milk, stirring constantly, then the Madeira, crabmeat, and salt to taste. Simmer 15 to 20 minutes without boiling. If the bisque is thicker than you'd like, stir in a little more milk to thin it. Serve hot.

Stock

4 cups chicken stock

2 cups water

¼ cup soy sauce

2 teaspoons sesame oil

2 tablespoons sambal oelek

2 tablespoons minced garlic

2 tablespoons diced green onion
   bulbs (green parts reserved
   and sliced thinly for garnish)

2 tablespoons sugar

Duck wontons

4 ounces duck breast, skin removed

1 tablespoon soy sauce

½ teaspoon sesame oil

Pinch sesame seeds

¼ cup panko bread crumbs

24 to 26 wonton wrappers

1 (4-ounce) package wonton crisps,
   for garnish

Serves 8 to 12

Duck Wonton Soup

THE STICKY ELBOW, WILLIAMSPORT
MANAGER JASON MATTY

*This duck wonton soup is not at all fussy to put together—the process of
filling and assembling the wontons is oddly soothing. It packs a punch,
so you may need to adjust the sambal oelek to your liking.*

For the stock:
In a large stockpot, stir together the chicken stock, water, soy sauce,
sesame oil, sambal oelek, minced garlic, green onions, and sugar and
bring to a boil. Simmer while you prepare the wontons.

For the duck wontons:
In a food processor, pulse together the duck breast, soy sauce, sesame
oil, and sesame seeds until well combined. Transfer to a medium
bowl and add the panko, mixing by hand.

Wet the edges of a wonton wrapper and put a little filling in the
middle. Gather the edges together in a bunch and press to seal.
Repeat with remaining wonton wrappers until all the filling is used.

Bring the stock back to a boil, drop in the wontons, and boil for
5 minutes. Ladle a few wontons and some stock into bowls and
garnish with fried wonton crisps and the green parts of scallions.
Serve immediately.

½ cup (1 stick) butter

1 cup flour

4 cups ham or pork stock

2 cups smashed cooked
    great northern beans

2 cups whole cooked
    great northern beans

2 cups diced ham steak
    or ham hocks

1½ teaspoons granulated garlic

⅛ teaspoon cayenne pepper

1 teaspoon salt

½ teaspoon white pepper

½ teaspoon onion powder

1 tablespoon Worcestershire sauce

½ cup chopped fresh parsley,
    for garnish

Serves 6 to 8

Fairfield Inn
Ham and Bean Soup

THE HISTORIC FAIRFIELD INN, FAIRFIELD
HEAD CHEF JOHNATHON MCGRAIN

When Robert E. Lee led his army from northern Virginia through Fairfield in July 1863, the Fairfield innkeepers and local women from town served the tired and hungry soldiers this meal. The recipe has been handed down from innkeeper to innkeeper since then. If you can't find granulated garlic, use garlic powder. The innkeepers recommend a semi-sweet red wine to go with this soup.

Melt the butter in a large stockpot over medium-high heat. Slowly add the flour, whisking constantly to make a roux. Cook for 2 minutes, being careful to not burn it. Gradually add the ham stock, whisking constantly to prevent the roux from clumping. Bring to a boil, stirring periodically, until the stock starts to thicken.

Add the smashed great northern beans, breaking up any large clumps. Add the whole great northern beans and diced ham and continue to boil for 4 minutes.

Reduce the heat to simmer. Add the garlic, cayenne pepper, salt, white pepper, onion powder, and Worcestershire sauce.

Continue to simmer for 1 hour. Garnish with parsley and more salt and pepper, if desired.

4 cups water

6 cherrystone clams

1 pound Yukon Gold potatoes,
½-inch dice

4 tablespoons butter

¾ cup ¼-inch dice Spanish onion

¾ cup ¼-inch dice celery

1 garlic clove, smashed

1½ teaspoons Wondra flour

20 cockles or littleneck clams

1 cup heavy cream

2 tablespoons chopped
fresh parsley

Kosher salt and white pepper

Serves 6 to 8

New England Clam Chowder

3RD & FERRY FISH MARKET, EASTON
CHEF-OWNER MIKE PICHETTO

In part because of its "keystone" location, Pennsylvania borrows freely from neighboring regions. A classic take on a New England staple, this chowder is flavorful and remarkably light despite the fact that it contains heavy cream. Wondra flour, found in the baking aisle of most supermarkets, is the secret for a smooth texture.

In a large stockpot, bring the water to a boil and add the cherrystone clams. Boil until the clams open; this should only take a couple of minutes, so keep an eye on them. Remove the clams from the water, extract the meat, and chop roughly into pieces. Set clams aside; discard the shells.

Strain the clam cooking liquid through a fine-mesh sieve to remove any sand from the clams (you may need to do this twice). Return the liquid to the stockpot, add the diced potatoes, and simmer until tender, 15 to 20 minutes. Strain the liquid again and remove the cooked potatoes. Reserve the cooking liquid.

In a separate stockpot, melt the butter and add the onion, celery, and garlic, sautéing until aromatic, about 2 minutes. Stir in the Wondra flour.

Add the reserved clam cooking liquid to the second stockpot and bring to a boil. Add the cockles or littleneck clams and cook until they start to open. Add the cream and return to a boil. Reduce the temperature to a simmer and add the chopped cherrystones and cooked potatoes. Return to a boil briefly and adjust the seasoning to taste with the parsley, kosher salt, and white pepper. Serve hot with oyster crackers.

Soy-marinated mushrooms

2 cups hen of the woods mushrooms

2 cups shiitake mushrooms

2 cups crimini mushrooms

2 cups royal trumpet mushrooms

1 tablespoon vegetable oil

1 tablespoon minced shallots

1 teaspoon minced fresh ginger

1 teaspoon minced fresh garlic

1 scallion, green and white
      parts sliced thin

1 to 2 tablespoons sherry vinegar

1 to 2 tablespoons soy sauce

Mushroom tare

2 tablespoons minced soy-marinated
      mushrooms

1 tablespoon minced shallot

1 teaspoon minced fresh ginger

1 teaspoon minced garlic

2 scallions, sliced very thin
      and minced

1 tablespoon soy sauce

1 tablespoon sherry vinegar

½ teaspoon sesame oil

1 tablespoon miso paste

1 teaspoon lemon juice

Pennsylvania Mushroom Ramen

MISTER LEE'S NOODLES, EASTON
CHEF-OWNER LEE CHIZMAR

The secret to amazing ramen? Layers of flavor. Add kosher salt, to taste, after assembling each element. Chef Chizmar recommends Sun Noodles (see Sources, page 138).

For the soy-marinated mushrooms:
Destem and thinly slice all the mushrooms; reserve the stems. In a large sauté pan, heat the oil over high heat to just smoking, then add all the mushrooms. Sauté over high heat, tossing every 30 seconds until the liquid from the mushrooms has cooked off, and then season with salt. Continue to cook until the mushrooms begin to caramelize and turn golden brown, about 5 minutes. Reduce the heat to medium and add the shallots, ginger, garlic, and scallion. Sauté for 3 minutes, being careful not to burn. Deglaze the pan with the sherry vinegar and soy sauce to taste. Adjust the seasoning and remove from heat. Cook a day in advance and reheat before serving.

For the mushroom tare:
A day in advance, combine all the ingredients in a small lidded container, cover, and refrigerate.

For the mushroom-marinated tofu:
Place the diced tofu in a medium bowl. In a small bowl or 1-quart measuring cup, whisk together the stock, soy sauce, and vinegar, then pour over the tofu. Marinade at least 12 hours and up to 72 hours in the refrigerator.

(continued on page 68)

Mushroom-marinated tofu

1 block extra-firm tofu,
    pressed for 24 hours,
    then 1½ inch diced

1 cup mushroom stock

1 cup soy sauce

½ cup rice wine vinegar

Mushroom dashi (broth)

1 tablespoon vegetable oil

4 cups crimini mushrooms

Reserved mushroom stems
    from soy-marinated mushrooms

1 Spanish onion, julienned

4 garlic cloves, sliced thin

2 stalks celery, sliced thin on bias

1 leek, washed and sliced thin

1 jalapeño, deseeded and sliced thin

2 shallots, julienned

1 ounce fresh ginger, sliced thin

¼ bunch fresh thyme

1 teaspoon kosher salt

1 cup soy sauce

3 quarts cold water

2 cups bonito flakes

1 teaspoon sesame oil

1 tablespoon sherry vinegar

1 (12-inch) piece kombu (kelp)

1 tablespoon fresh lemon juice

For the mushroom dashi:
Heat the vegetable oil in a stockpot over medium heat and add the crimini mushrooms and stems reserved from the soy-marinated mushrooms. Stir until the mushrooms begin to soften, 5 to 8 minutes. Add the onion, garlic, celery, leek, jalapeño, shallots, ginger, thyme, and salt and cook, stirring frequently, for 10 to 15 minutes.

Deglaze the pan with soy sauce and simmer, reducing the liquid by half. Add the cold water and simmer for 30 minutes to 1 hour. Remove from the heat and add the bonito flakes, sesame oil, sherry vinegar, kombu, and lemon juice. Steep for 10 minutes, strain through a fine-mesh sieve, and discard the vegetables and other solids.

For the ramen:
Follow the package instructions to cook the ramen. Place 1 teaspoon mushroom tare and 1 teaspoon blended vegetable oil (garlic oil if you have it) in the bottom of each bowl. Add a portion of cooked ramen. Add a couple of ladles of hot mushroom dashi and slightly agitate the noodles. Work your way around each bowl, garnishing with soy-marinated mushrooms, tofu, and a poached egg. Top with thinly sliced scallions. Serve immediately.

Ramen

1 (12-ounce) package Sun Noodles ramen

4 to 6 teaspoons blended vegetable oil

4 to 6 poached eggs

⅓ cup chopped scallions, for garnish

Serves 4 to 6

1 ⅓ cups chopped onions

2 to 3 tablespoons butter or oil

4 cups deseeded, peeled,
    and chopped long neck squash

2 cups peeled and chopped
    sweet potato

¼ cup chopped fresh ginger

1 teaspoon kosher salt

1 teaspoon freshly cracked
    black pepper

½ teaspoon cinnamon

⅛ teaspoon ground allspice

⅛ teaspoon ground cardamom

⅛ teaspoon ground nutmeg

2 fresh sage leaves, chopped

4 to 6 cups water or chicken stock,
    just enough to cover

2 cups heavy cream

½ cup sour cream, sprinkled
    with cinnamon, for garnish

Serves 6 to 8

Pumpkin, Sweet Potato, and Ginger Bisque

JOHN J. JEFFRIES RESTAURANT, LANCASTER
CHEF-OWNER MICHAEL F. CARSON

From Lancaster's most popular farm-to-table restaurant, this root vegetable soup offers the best of fall and winter in its subtle balance of sweet and spicy that's sure to warm you as the weather turns colder. This recipe works best with Pennsylvania long neck squash—also known as neck pumpkin—because they are sweeter. Although technically not a pumpkin, it imbues this dish with autumnal orange hues.

In a large stockpot, sweat the onions with butter or oil until soft, 5 to 7 minutes.

Add the squash and sweet potato, then the ginger, salt, pepper, cinnamon, allspice, cardamom, nutmeg, and sage. Add enough liquid to barely cover the vegetables. Bring to a boil, cover, and reduce to simmer until the vegetables are just soft, 15 to 20 minutes. Stir occasionally to prevent sticking.

Once the vegetables have softened, add the cream and gently heat. Puree the soup with an immersion blender (or pour into a blender and puree). If desired, strain through a sieve for a smoother soup.

Garnish with a dollop of the cinnamon-spiked sour cream and serve hot.

Roasted Kennett Square Mushroom Soup

PORTABELLO'S, KENNETT SQUARE
CHEF-OWNER BRETT HULBERT

Kennett Square is well known for being the mushroom capital of the United States, producing upwards of a million pounds of them every week. This soup is always on the menu at Portabello's. Don't be put off by the unusual method: yes, you are making soup in the oven. Freeze any leftovers and, after thawing, add fresh milk or cream while reheating for the desired consistency.

2 pounds shiitake mushrooms,
    stems discarded and caps sliced

2 pounds white mushrooms,
    roughly chopped into
    large pieces

½ cup extra virgin olive oil

1 teaspoon kosher salt

1 ½ teaspoons freshly
    ground black pepper

½ cup chopped shallots

1 garlic clove, peeled

2 tablespoons rice flour

½ cup Madeira wine

3 cups chicken broth

1 ½ cups beef broth

½ cup heavy whipping cream

1 tablespoon chopped fresh thyme

1 tablespoon chopped fresh sage

1 cup water

½ cup chopped scallions,
    green parts only

Preheat the oven to 400 degrees. Place a rack on the lowest shelf in the oven.

Place mushrooms in one or two large, deep roasting pans. Drizzle olive oil over the mushrooms and toss to coat. Sprinkle with salt and pepper. Roast in the oven for 20 minutes, then remove and add the shallots and whole garlic clove. Dust evenly with flour to avoid clumps and stir to combine. Return the pan to the oven and roast another 10 minutes.

Remove the roasting pan from the oven. Stir in the Madeira along with the chicken and beef broths, cream, thyme, and sage. Return the pan to the oven and let simmer for 15 to 20 minutes. Remove the pan from the oven and transfer all but one-quarter of the soup to a large serving bowl.

Use an immersion blender to puree the main bowl of soup (or puree in a blender). Pour the remaining quarter of the soup into the bowl and stir. Taste for seasoning; if it's too salty, add water and reheat. Ladle into soup bowls and garnish with chopped scallions.

Serves 8

Beverages

Moscow Miel, p. 81

Rosemary simple syrup

3 to 4 rosemary sprigs

1 cup water

1 cup sugar

Cocktail

2 ounces Eight Oaks Applejack

4 ounces Colony Meadery
    Tea Tax Mead

2 ounces rosemary simple syrup

Makes 1 cocktail

Apple of My Eye

THE COLONY MEADERY, ALLENTOWN
TASTING ROOM MANAGER DAVE MCADOO

Mead, made from fermented honey, has a long history, dating back at least 4,000 years. This cocktail incorporates Tea Tax mead from The Colony Meadery and is infused with black tea and lemon. Eight Oaks Craft Distillers in New Tripoli uses local fruit from Scholl Orchards in Kempton for their Applejack. You can order both of these items online, all year long.

For the rosemary simple syrup:
Wash and pat dry the rosemary with a paper towel. Rosemary tends to gather dirt easily, so do your best to remove what you can.

In a small pot over medium heat, bring the rosemary, water, and sugar to a boil. Let it boil for a minute while stirring until the sugar dissolves. Remove from the heat and let steep for 30 minutes. Remove the sprigs.

Using a fine-mesh sieve, strain the simple syrup several times until it's mostly clear; you may see small particulates floating around. If that bothers you, strain a final time with cheesecloth into a glass measuring cup.

For the cocktail:
Fill a shaker halfway with ice and add the Applejack, mead, and syrup. Cover and shake well. Traditionally, this drink is served in a pilsner or Renaissance glass, but if you don't have either of those, an Old Fashioned or other tumbler will also work.

Bloody Mary mix

3 cups tomato juice

2 teaspoons horseradish

1½ teaspoons Tabasco sauce

1 tablespoon Worcestershire sauce

Juice of 1 large lemon

2 teaspoons celery salt

2 teaspoons black pepper

2 teaspoons mustard powder

2 teaspoons granulated garlic

2 tablespoons olive juice

Cocktail

Enough ice to fill four
    14-ounce glasses

1 teaspoon lemon juice

1 teaspoon Old Bay® Seasoning

6 ounces Barrel 21 vodka

24 ounces Bloody Mary mix

4 leafy celery stalks, for garnish

4 lemon twists, for garnish

8 olives, for garnish

Makes 4 cocktails

Barrel 21 Bloody Mary

BARREL 21 DISTILLERY & DINING, STATE COLLEGE
MANAGER BEN BULLOCK

Barrel 21 is owned by the same people who have been operating the land-mark Otto's Pub and Brewery in State College for many years. This cocktail takes just a few minutes to put together and is a savory eye-opener. It's also a well-loved offering of Barrel 21's award-winning brunch—they have an actual Bloody Mary bar.

For the Bloody Mary mix:
In a large pitcher, combine the tomato juice, horseradish, Tabasco and Worcestershire sauces, lemon juice, salt and spices, and olive juice. Stir to blend.

For the cocktail:
Squeeze the lemon juice into a small bowl, enough to coat the rim of the serving glasses. Add Old Bay® Seasoning into a second small bowl. Rim a 14-ounce glass with the lemon juice and then dip it into the Old Bay® Seasoning to coat. Fill the glass with ice and add 1½ ounces of Barrel 21 vodka. Add 6 ounces of Bloody Mary mix and garnish with a piece of leafy celery, lemon twist, and two olives on a skewer. Repeat with three more glasses.

3 cups water

1 cup sugar

½ cup honey

1 tablespoon caraway seeds

4 whole cloves

6 sticks cinnamon

3 oranges, quartered

1 (1.75-liter) bottle inexpensive
Canadian whiskey

Makes 6 cups

Boilo Winter Punch

LEW BRYSON, NEWTOWN ❧ AUTHOR OF *TASTING WHISKEY*

Lew Bryson shared this unique winter punch that hails from St. Clair, the heart of the coal region. The tradition is to welcome guests from the cold with a warm glass of boilo, usually in mason jars. Don't bother with the good stuff—the nuances of a fine whiskey will be wasted. Pick a cheap Canadian one and you'll be doing it right. But in the words of the locals, remember—"Watch out, it can get you."

Place the water, sugar, honey, caraway seeds, cloves, and cinnamon in a large stockpot. Squeeze the oranges over the pot and then add them in as well. Bring to a boil and hold at a boil for 5 minutes. Remove the stockpot from the heat and stir in the whiskey. Return to heat, bring to a boil again, and immediately remove from the heat. Cover and cool at room temperature (or refrigerate) overnight.

Using a fine sieve, strain the boilo into a large glass Pyrex measuring cup. Remove the cinnamon sticks from the pot and put them into clean mason jars. Pour the boilo into the jars and cap them. The lore is that "rusty lids add character," so don't go out and buy new ones if you've got some on hand. This is as homey and straightforward as it gets.

❧ **Note:** *Boilo is delicious when you reheat it with some apple cider; it also cuts it a bit, if you find it's too strong. Boilo makes a great gift.*

Maple, sage, and thyme simple syrup

1 cup water

5 sage leaves

5 sprigs thyme

½ cup granulated sugar

½ cup maple syrup

Cocktail

2 ounces Wigle Barrel
  Rested Ginever

½ ounce maple, sage, and thyme
  simple syrup

6 dashes Wigle Rosemary
  Lavender Bitters

Lemon twist, for garnish

Sprigs of seasonal fresh herbs,
  for garnish

Makes 1 cocktail

The Botanist

WIGLE WHISKEY, PITTSBURGH
BARRELHOUSE AND COCKTAIL PROGRAM MANAGER AUDRA KELLY

All summer long, the staff at Wigle Whiskey, a certified organic distillery, makes variations on this botanically driven drink. This particular iteration calls for a simple syrup infused with maple, sage, and thyme. Up the ante by using your favorite bitters; Wigle makes its own. You can order it online (see Sources, page 138).

For the maple, sage, and thyme simple syrup:
In a small saucepan, boil the water, then remove from heat and steep the sage and thyme for 10 minutes. Add the sugar and maple syrup and stir to dissolve. Strain the syrup through a fine-mesh sieve into an airtight container. The syrup can be stored for up to a month in the refrigerator.

For the cocktail:
In a large mixing glass, stir together the ginever, simple syrup, and bitters and pour into a glass with a large ice cube. Garnish with a lemon twist and any seasonal fresh herbs you have on hand.

Simple syrup

2 cups water

1 cup sugar

Cocktail

2 ounces Dad's Hat
    Pennsylvania Rye Whiskey

1 ounce lemon juice

¾ ounce simple syrup

1 egg white (optional)

1 maraschino cherry, for garnish

Makes 1 cocktail

Dad's Hat Whiskey Sour

DAD'S HAT, BRISTOL
CO-FOUNDER, MOUNTAIN LAUREL SPIRITS, JOHN COOPER

Once upon a time—specifically, before Prohibition—Pennsylvania was home to 163 licensed distilleries producing rye whiskey. In fact, the state basically was the "emperor, king, and queen" of rye whiskey, says Cooper. Dad's Hat was the first new distillery to pop up since Prohibition.

For the simple syrup:
In a small saucepan boil the water, add the sugar, and stir to dissolve. Remove from heat, let cool, and pour into an airtight container. The syrup can be stored for up to a month in the refrigerator.

For the cocktail:
For a velvety-smooth drink with a foamy cap, start with a shaker—but no ice. Add the rye whiskey, lemon juice, simple syrup, and egg white and shake. Then add ice, shake vigorously, and strain into a cocktail glass. (If you're not using the egg white, fill the shaker with ice, then add the ingredients and shake.) Garnish with a cherry and serve.

Regular menu version

4 ounces milk

1 banana

2 tablespoons peanut butter

2 teaspoons cacao or cocoa powder

2 teaspoons honey

1 tablespoon chia seeds

½ cup ice

"Secret" menu version

2 ounces cold brew coffee
    (or simply cold coffee)

2 ounces unsweetened
    vanilla coconut milk

1 scoop chocolate protein powder

1 banana

2 tablespoons dry peanut powder

2 tablespoons chia seeds

½ cup ice

Makes 1 smoothie

Elvis Smoothie

KATHY'S CAFÉ, HUGHESVILLE
OWNERS TRACY AND ANDY CLAYTON

Kathy's Café is like a diner, but much more interesting. The Elvis Smoothie is a best seller on the menu, but there's also a "secret" menu version of it, too, which makes it a bit healthier. Either way, it's delicious and named for the flavor combinations Elvis Presley loved.

Regardless of which version you make, simply combine all the ingredients in a high-speed blender and process until smooth. Pour into a tall glass and enjoy!

Ginger simple syrup

2 cups water

1 cup sugar

¼ cup fresh ginger, sliced
    thinly into rounds

Cocktail

½ ounce freshly squeezed
    lemon juice

2 ounces ginger simple syrup

2 ounces vodka

1 spoonful orange marmalade

Club soda

Freshly grated nutmeg, for garnish

Orange twist, for garnish

Makes 1 cocktail

Lady Marmalade

SOCIAL STILL DISTILLERY AND RESTAURANT, BETHLEHEM
OWNER ADAM FLATT

Adam Flatt, who operates this distillery and restaurant, is the son of Elaine Pivinski, who owns the award-winning Franklin Hill Vineyards north of Easton. This recipe is for one of Social Still's most popular cocktails, using their award-winning vodka.

For the ginger simple syrup:
In a medium pot, bring the water to a boil and stir in the sugar until it's dissolved. Add the sliced ginger and bring to a simmer. Remove from the heat and let steep for about 30 minutes. Strain through a fine-mesh sieve into an airtight container. Refrigerate for up to a month.

For the cocktail:
In a shaker, combine the lemon juice, ginger simple syrup, vodka, and marmalade. Add ice, cover, and shake. Pour into a stemless wine glass and top with a splash of club soda. Finish with freshly grated nutmeg and a twist of orange.

Ice chips

4 ounces Laurel Highlands
    Ginger Mead

1½ ounces Faber vodka

2 ounces ginger beer

Juice of ½ lime

Splash club soda or tonic water

Lime twist, for garnish

Makes 1 cocktail

Moscow Miel

LAUREL HIGHLANDS MEADERY, IRWIN
OWNERS MATT AND MANDY FALENSKI

Mead has a long history in Pennsylvania—it's a fermented honey beverage that was popular in colonial days. Laurel Highlands serves this drink, a spin on the Moscow Mule, during special events in its tasting room. They use Faber vodka from a local distillery that uses corn. For the finish, Matt prefers tonic water, but his wife Mandy prefers club soda.

Place the ice chips in a copper mug or other metal cup. Pour in the mead, vodka, ginger beer, lime juice, and club soda or tonic water. Stir once and garnish with a slice of lime.

Demerara syrup

2 cups raw Demerara
(turbinado) sugar

1 cup water

Cocktail

2 ounces Wigle Deep Cut
Rye Whiskey

½ ounce Grand Marnier

¼ ounce Demerara syrup

2 dashes coffee bitters

Orange twist, for garnish

Makes 1 cocktail

Salinger's Sling

BUTCHER AND THE RYE, PITTSBURGH
BEVERAGE DIRECTOR, RICHARD DESHANTZ RESTAURANT GROUP,
CECIL USHER

Butcher and the Rye, a 2015 semifinalist for the James Beard Foundation Outstanding Bar Program Award, created this tasty riff on the Old Fashioned. Spicier and more complex than its inspiration, this tipple sips as an ode to the era in which Salinger penned his famous novel—and calls for a local whiskey, to boot.

For the Demerara syrup:
Combine the sugar and water in a small saucepan and simmer over low heat, stirring occasionally, until the sugar dissolves. Transfer the syrup to an airtight container and store in the refrigerator for up to 1 month.

For the cocktail:
In a mixing glass with large ice cubes, add the rye whiskey, Grand Marnier, Demerara syrup, and coffee bitters and stir quickly. Strain over a large ice cube into a chilled Old Fashioned glass.

Twist the orange peel into a spiral (this brings out the essential oils) and rub over the rim of the glass. Place the peel on top of the drink and enjoy!

Main Courses

Braised Short Rib Poutine, p. 88

4 center-cut boneless pork chops
(about 1½ pounds)

Kosher salt and freshly ground
black pepper

4 garlic cloves, minced

Juice of 1 lime

¼ cup chopped fresh basil,
plus 2 tablespoons for garnish

⅓ cup almonds

4 peaches, halved

2 tablespoons olive oil

⅓ cup bleu cheese crumbles

Coarsely ground black pepper

Honey, for garnish

Serves 4

Basil-Marinated Pork Chops
with Grilled Peaches

BILL SELL'S BOLD, ALTOONA   ❧   CHEF-OWNER BILL SELL

At his namesake restaurant, Bill Sell does indeed love bold flavor. This entrée is best with summer's ripest peaches—a perfect foil for the honey, cheese, and almonds.

Rub the pork chops with salt and pepper and place them in a zip-top plastic bag. Add the minced garlic, lime juice, and ¼ cup of basil and let marinate for at least 30 minutes.

Using either a grill or a stovetop grill pan, cook the chops until their internal temperature reaches 160 degrees, 10 to 15 minutes; set aside.

Toast the almonds in a skillet over medium heat until fragrant, 5 to 7 minutes. Remove from the pan, let cool, then roughly chop.

Brush the peach halves with oil and grill, cut side down, for a few minutes. Remove from the grill, cut the halves lengthwise in half again, and plate with the pork. Top with the bleu cheese crumbles, toasted almonds, torn basil, and black pepper. Drizzle the plate with honey and serve immediately.

2¾ cups tipo 00 flour

1 teaspoon salt

¼ cup plus 2 tablespoons
    finely chopped basil

1 tablespoon extra virgin olive oil

13 large egg yolks

¼ cup water, as needed

½ cup freshly grated
    Parmesan cheese

Serves 4

Basil Pappardelle

NOTE BISTRO & WINE BAR, HARRISBURG
EXECUTIVE CHEF MATT ROSSI

Pappardelle is a rewarding homemade pasta. It's rich, eggy, and can be made without any fancy equipment—just your hands and a knife or pizza cutter to slice the pasta into ribbons. (If you have a pasta attachment for a KitchenAid stand mixer, use setting 5.) Wait for summer's basil; it works the best here. Most supermarkets carry tipo 00 flour, which has a finer grind, but all-purpose flour also works.

Combine the flour, salt, and ¼ cup of the basil in a mixing bowl or the bowl of a stand mixer with a dough hook. Make a well in the center of the flour and add the olive oil and egg yolks.

Combine all ingredients thoroughly until a firm dough forms. Add water as needed to bring the dough together. Transfer the dough to a floured surface and knead with force for 15 to 20 minutes to activate the gluten. Allow to rest at room temperature for 1 hour.

Either hand roll with a rolling pin or use the mixer pasta attachment to roll dough to roughly ⅛-inch thickness. Using a sharp knife or pizza cutter, hand cut the dough into 14-inch-long pieces, roughly ¾ inch wide.

In a large pot of salted boiling water, cook the pasta until al dente, 3 to 4 minutes. Drain and serve immediately, garnished with the remaining 2 tablespoons of basil and Parmesan cheese.

2 pounds pork cheeks

2 tablespoons kosher salt

2 tablespoons black pepper

4 tablespoons canola oil

3 cups 2-inch dice Spanish onions

2 cups 2-inch dice carrots

2 cups 2-inch dice celery

3 cups Victory Festbier or similar
German malt-driven beer

3 cups chicken stock

3 to 4 ounces (½ can) chipotle
peppers in adobo

8 tortilla shells

2 medium tomatoes, sliced thin

1 cup queso fresco

2 cups shredded cabbage

½ cup chopped fresh cilantro

Serves 6 to 8

Braised Pork Cheek Tacos

VICTORY BREWING COMPANY, DOWNINGTON
EXECUTIVE CHEF GLENN MCQUEEN

If you can't find pork cheeks at your local grocery store or butcher, try a small (about three pounds) pork shoulder instead and use the leftover pork in more tacos, a pot of chili, or smothered in St. Louis Barbecue Sauce (see page 133 in Cook's Pantry).

Preheat the oven to 250 degrees. Season the pork cheeks evenly with salt and pepper.

Over medium-high heat, pour the oil into a large skillet and let it heat to nearly smoking; a drop of water will sizzle. Sear the pork cheeks for a couple of minutes on each side. Once the pork cheeks are well browned, remove them from the skillet and place in a deep baking dish.

Using the same skillet, cook the onions, carrots, and celery until the onions are translucent (about 5 minutes) and then layer them over the pork cheeks.

Pour the beer, chicken stock, and peppers over the pork cheeks. The liquid should come about three-quarters of the way up the pork cheeks.

Cover the baking dish with aluminum foil and cook for 4 hours. The pork cheeks are fully cooked when you are able to pull the meat easily apart with a fork.

Remove the pork from the baking dish, break up the meat, and distribute among your favorite tortilla shells. Top with sliced tomatoes, queso fresco, shredded cabbage, and cilantro and serve immediately.

❧ **Note:** *Save the cooking liquid to use when reheating any leftovers. Using a fine-mesh sieve, strain the braising liquid and discard the vegetables. Place the strained liquid in a medium-sized pot and bring to a low simmer, reducing by three-quarters. Let cool, then pour into a lidded container and refrigerate. Reheat the pork cheeks in the reduction in a saucepan over medium-low heat.*

Short ribs

¾ to 1 pound bone-in short ribs

Salt and black pepper

2 tablespoons canola or
grape seed oil

1 medium white onion,
roughly chopped

2 stalks celery, roughly chopped

1 carrot, roughly chopped

4 garlic cloves

5 sprigs fresh thyme

½ bunch fresh parsley

2 teaspoons black peppercorns

¼ cup tomato paste

¾ cup beef stock

2 tablespoons cornstarch

2 cups brown ale, porter or lager

Poutine

1 pound french fried potatoes,
tossed in sea salt and finely
chopped fresh rosemary

2 tablespoons canola or other oil

1 small white onion, sliced
into half-moons

6 ounces Cheddar cheese
curds or mozzarella

2 to 3 tablespoons chopped fresh
chives or green parts of scallions

Serves 2

Braised Short Rib Poutine

TWO RIVERS BREWING COMPANY, EASTON
EXECUTIVE CHEF JEREMY BIALKER

Hearty and filling, poutine is comforting enough on its own, but short ribs make the dish savory. The recipe serves two generously, but you could easily double it and braise it in a larger pot. Serve this with homemade french fries (use Yukon Gold potatoes) or good-quality frozen ones.

For the short ribs:
Preheat the oven to 300 degrees. Pat the beef dry and coat with salt and pepper.

Heat the oil over high in a large skillet. Brown the ribs on all sides, about 15 minutes total. Remove from the pan and set aside.

Reduce the heat to medium and add the onion, celery, carrot, garlic, thyme, parsley, and peppercorns. Cook the vegetables until caramelized, about 15 minutes. Add the tomato paste and cook another 5 minutes.

Whisk together the beef stock and cornstarch until combined. Add the beef back to the pan along with the beef stock and beer and simmer until reduced by one-third. Cover the pan with foil or a lid and braise in the oven until fork tender, about 2 hours.

Remove the lid and cook another 20 minutes. Remove the beef. Strain the sauce, return it to the pan, and reduce by one-quarter. After the meat has cooled enough to handle, pull it apart, removing the large chunks of fat, but leaving a few for flavor and texture.

For the poutine:
Cook the french fries in the oven according to the package directions.

Meanwhile, heat the oil in a skillet over medium heat and add the onions. Cook until caramelized, 15 to 20 minutes. Set aside.

Heat a cast-iron skillet in a 350-degree oven until hot. Remove from the oven and add the fries. Place the short ribs, cheese curds, caramelized onions, and drippings from the onion pan into the skillet and put it in the oven for about 5 minutes—you want the cheese to melt but not brown. Remove from the oven and top with a little more pan drippings along with freshly cracked black pepper and the chives or scallions. Serve hot.

1½ to 2 pounds boneless chicken
    breasts (or thighs)

½ cup flour

½ teaspoon kosher salt

Pinch black pepper

3 tablespoons grated
    Parmesan cheese

4 tablespoons olive oil

4 to 6 tablespoons butter, divided

¾ cup Merry Monks
    or other Belgian tripel

¼ cup lemon juice

¼ cup capers, undrained

¼ cup chopped fresh parsley,
    for garnish

Serves 4 to 6

Chicken Piccata with
Merry Monks Reduction

WEYERBACHER BREWING COMPANY, EASTON
NATIONAL ACCOUNTS MANAGER ANDY COULSEY

*A familiar dish gets a twist from the award-winning Merry Monks beer,
a Belgian-style tripel known not only for its high ABV (9.3 percent) but
even more for its well-balanced taste (bananas, pears, slightly spicy note)
and dry finish.*

Wash the chicken and pat it dry. Slice the breasts in half horizontally,
especially if they are thick. Wrap in plastic or put in a zip-top bag
and pound with the back of a wooden spoon or a meat tenderizer
to approximately ¼-inch thickness. Set aside.

Preheat the oven to 225 degrees. In a small, shallow bowl, mix the
flour, salt, pepper, and grated Parmesan. Dredge each piece of chicken
in the flour mixture until well coated.

Heat the olive oil and 2 tablespoons of the butter in a large skillet
on medium-high heat. Add chicken one or two slices at a time,
resisting the urge to crowd the skillet. Cook about 3 minutes per
side, adding more butter if needed. Remove the chicken from the
skillet, place on a heat-safe plate, and cover with aluminum foil.
Place in the preheated oven to keep warm.

Over medium heat, add the beer, lemon juice, and capers to the
same skillet, using a spatula to scrape up the browned bits. Simmer
the sauce, reducing by a third to a half. Whisk in the remaining
2 tablespoons of butter.

Remove the chicken from the oven and plate it with the sauce
poured on top. Sprinkle with parsley and serve with rice or roasted
potatoes.

Cornmeal Parisian Gnocchi

NOTE BISTRO & WINE BAR, HARRISBURG
EXECUTIVE CHEF MATT ROSSI

At Note—a Mediterranean-leaning spot in an old Victorian building—this cornmeal gnocchi is just one of several components of a dish that features wild boar. However, the gnocchi is so good on its own that it works as a meal by itself.

2 cups water

1 cup (2 sticks) butter

½ teaspoon kosher salt

1½ cups flour

1 cup finely ground cornmeal

6 large eggs

1 tablespoon minced garlic

¼ cup chopped fresh parsley, divided

1 cup grated Grana Padano cheese

Freshly ground black pepper

Serves 4

Combine the water, butter, and salt in a large pot. Bring to a rapid boil over high heat. Add the flour and cornmeal and rapidly whisk until it is thoroughly combined into a thick batter. Transfer to a mixing bowl and allow to cool slightly.

Using a whisk or the paddle attachment on a stand mixer, incorporate the eggs, one at a time, until the dough comes together. Add the garlic, 2 tablespoons of parsley, and the cheese and mix until evenly distributed. Transfer to a piping bag. Refrigerate for up to an hour if the dough feels soft.

Bring a large pot of water to boil. Pipe out 1-inch pieces and cut them right into the boiling water with a knife. Gnocchi are finished cooking when they float and puff up slightly; it should take a couple of minutes. (If you aren't sure, take a gnocchi out and cut through the middle—if the cornmeal is dark yellow, it isn't done yet.)

Transfer to waiting plates, sprinkle with more cheese, black pepper, and the remaining chopped parsley.

⋙ **Note:** *Cooked gnocchi will last for roughly 3 days in the refrigerator and 30 days in the freezer.*

Short ribs

2½ pounds meaty bone-in
   short ribs

Kosher salt

2 tablespoons olive oil

2 large yellow onions, diced large

1 carrot, diced large

1 (12-ounce) bottle of ale

2 cups beef stock or broth

12 peppercorns

2 leafy sprigs fresh rosemary

2 small bay leaves

1 cup fresh cranberries

Squash and Brussels sprouts

8 large Brussels sprouts

3 tablespoons olive oil

1 pound butternut squash
   (peeled, seeded,
   and diced large)

2 teaspoons chopped fresh thyme

Salt and black pepper

Cranberry Ale-Braised Short Ribs with Squash and Brussels Sprouts

SAVORY GRILLE, MACUNGIE   ∾   CHEF-OWNER SHAWN DOYLE

There are a few elements to this dish, but they're not complicated and come together fairly easily—much of the preparation can be taken care of while the short ribs braise. This dish celebrates the best of autumn from a restaurant that changes its menu in accordance with the cycle of the seasons.

For the short ribs:
Preheat the oven to 300 degrees.

Salt the short ribs. Heat the oil in a sauté pan and add only as many ribs as will fit without touching. Brown the ribs, turning with tongs, until chestnut-brown on all sides, about 4 minutes per side. Transfer the seared ribs to a roasting pan without stacking them, and continue until all the ribs are browned.

Pour off and discard all but about a tablespoon of fat from the sauté pan. Return the pan to medium-high heat and add the onions and carrot, stirring a few times until the vegetables start to brown and soften, about 5 minutes.

Add the ale, beef stock, peppercorns, rosemary, bay leaves, and cranberries to the sauté pan and bring to a boil. Pour the stock mixture over the short ribs, then set the lid securely in place and braise in the oven at a gentle simmer. Turn the ribs with tongs (so as not to tear up the meat) every 40 to 45 minutes and cook until fork-tender, about 2½ hours.

Remove the short ribs from the braising liquid and keep warm in the oven. Strain off the liquid from the vegetables and skim the fat from the liquid. Transfer the liquid to a saucepan and reduce over low heat to the consistency of a syrup.

Cranberry relish

1 cup fresh cranberries

½ cup water

¼ cup sugar

Zest from ½ orange

Serves 4

For the squash and Brussels sprouts:
Bring a medium saucepan of salted water to a boil. Drop the Brussels sprouts into the boiling water for 30 seconds. Remove the sprouts from the water and peel off the outside leaves. Drop leaves into a bowl of cold water with ice. Repeat four to five times, saving just the green outside leaves.

Heat the olive oil in a sauté pan over medium heat and add the butternut squash. Continuously stir the butternut until all sides turn an amber color, 10 to 15 minutes. Add the thyme, Brussels sprouts, and salt and pepper to taste.

For the cranberry relish:
Place the cranberries, water, sugar, and orange zest in a small saucepan and bring to a boil. Cook until the berries burst open, about 5 minutes. Place in a lidded container and refrigerate.

To assemble:
Place a short rib on a plate, then the squash and Brussels sprouts, and finish with a small dollop of cranberry relish. Drizzle the braising sauce on top and enjoy!

Linguini with Mussels and Peperonata

VETRI RESTAURANT GROUP, PHILADELPHIA
CHEF-FOUNDER MARC VETRI

The James Beard Award–winning chef and restaurateur Marc Vetri knows a thing or two about a good pasta dish. This deceptively simple linguini dish with several types of peppers creates layers of heat.

2 to 3 pounds mussels

1 tablespoon peppercorns

½ cup parsley stems

2 to 3 tablespoons grape seed or olive oil

1 onion, minced

2 red bell peppers, diced small

2 yellow bell peppers, diced small

3 Fresno peppers (or jalapeños), diced small

1 garlic clove, minced

1 cup white wine

1 tablespoon chili flakes

1 pound linguini

2 tablespoons chopped fresh parsley

1 tablespoon lemon juice

2 tablespoons butter

Serves 4 to 6

Rinse and clean the mussels. Wrap the peppercorns and parsley stems in cheesecloth to create a sachet and close it up with butcher's twine.

In a large, deep sauté pan, heat the oil over medium-high heat and sweat the onion, peppers, and garlic until they've softened, about 5 minutes. Add the white wine, chili flakes, and the peppercorn-parsley sachet, making a peperonata sauce. Bring to a boil.

Add the mussels and bring back to a boil. Cover and cook until the mussels open, 3 to 4 minutes.

Meanwhile, cook the linguini in salted boiling water according to the package directions.

Pour the peperonata sauce and mussels into a wide container to cool. Once cool, pick the mussels from the shells and set aside; discard shells. Return the sauce to the pan and reduce by half. Add the mussels back into the pan.

Add the pasta to the sauté pan and, over low heat, add the parsley, lemon juice, and butter and toss together, stirring vigorously at times, until the sauce is creamy. Serve immediately.

1 pound orzo pasta

4 tablespoons butter

¼ cup flour

1 cup heavy cream

2 cups 2% milk

½ cup water

1 teaspoon Worcestershire sauce

2 tablespoons Old Bay® Seasoning, divided

1½ tablespoons mustard powder

¾ pound Parmesan cheese

½ pound Boursin cheese

1 pound lump crabmeat

1 cup panko bread crumbs

Serves 8 to 10

Lump Crab Macaroni & Cheese

APOLLO GRILL, BETHLEHEM   ✖   CHEF JORDAN VAN WERT

Apollo is known for its extensive small bites/appetizer menu, but feel free to serve this hearty dish as an entrée. If you want to bake it in the oven in individual cast-iron skillets, keep the same temperature but reduce the time to eight to ten minutes.

Preheat the oven to 425 degrees.

Bring a large pot of salted water to a rapid bowl and cook the pasta according to the package directions. Drain and set aside. Do not rinse.

In a pot, melt the butter, add the flour, and stir over medium heat until the mixture bubbles. Add the heavy cream, milk, and water, bring to a slow boil, then lower the heat to simmer to make a roux. The mixture will become smooth and a bit thicker.

Add the Worcestershire sauce, 1 tablespoon of the Old Bay®, dry mustard, and Parmesan and Boursin cheeses. Stir to combine and turn the heat to low. Mix the lump crabmeat and cooked pasta into the cheese sauce. Place the mixture into a 4-quart oven–safe baking dish.

Toss together the panko bread crumbs and remaining 1 tablespoon Old Bay® in a small bowl. Sprinkle the panko over the top of the pasta and bake in the oven until golden brown and bubbling, about 30 minutes.

1 large tomato

3 to 4 pounds fresh mussels, washed and scrubbed

2 garlic cloves, minced

2 cups Shawnee Bière Blanche (or your favorite wheat beer)

1 tablespoon finely chopped fresh parsley

1 teaspoon finely chopped fresh thyme

2 tablespoons salted butter

Serves 4

Mussels in Bière Blanche

SHAWNEE INN AND GOLF RESORT, SHAWNEE ON DELAWARE
EXECUTIVE CHEF DEAN GARDNER

Shawnee Inn is unusual in that it's a golf resort with its own craft brewery. These mussels simmer in Shawnee's Bière Blanche, but any good wheat beer will do.

Cut a cross at the bottom of the tomato with a paring knife. Submerse the tomato in boiling water until the skin begins to separate, about 45 seconds. Remove the tomato and place it in a bowl of ice water. Let cool.

Remove the tomato from the ice bath and gently remove the skin. Quarter the tomato and then remove the center and the seeds. The meaty part of the tomato with no seed or skin is the *concassé*. Dice and reserve.

Wash and scrub the mussels and place them in a deep, wide saucepan (or stockpot) over medium heat. Add the garlic and beer. Cover and steam until the mussels open, 3 to 5 minutes.

Add the parsley, thyme, tomato concassé, and butter to the mussels. Continue to cook, uncovered, another 2 to 3 minutes to blend the flavors and slightly reduce the broth.

Serve in a bowl with the broth, along with your favorite bread or rolls for dipping.

Old Forge-Style Pizza

CARRIE HAVRANEK, THE DHARMA KITCHEN

In the coal regions of northeastern Pennsylvania, in the town of Old Forge, they make a certain kind of pizza. Rather than a pie, people call it a tray. It's square, but it's not a Sicilian pizza. This recipe isn't meant to create an exact replica, but it's inspired by the Old Forge approach and the Italian families who settled there.

2 packets active dry yeast

1 cup water, lukewarm, divided

2½ cups sifted flour

¼ cup vegetable oil

1 teaspoon salt

1 teaspoon sugar

1 sweet onion, diced

4 tablespoons olive oil, divided

2 tablespoons tomato paste

1 (28-ounce) can whole tomatoes,
    peeled

Salt and black pepper

4 slices American cheese

1 cup shredded white Cheddar

1 cup shredded mozzarella cheese

Serves 2 to 4

Combine the yeast and half of the water in the bowl of a stand mixer and let sit until it becomes foamy, about 5 minutes. Add the flour, vegetable oil, salt, and sugar and the rest of the water and bring the dough together until it's smooth but slightly sticky, about 5 minutes.

Let the dough rest in an oiled bowl in a warm spot for about an hour, covered. It should double in bulk. Preheat the oven to 450 degrees.

In a small saucepan over medium heat, cook the diced onion in 2 tablespoons of the olive oil until translucent, about 10 minutes. Add the tomato paste and the whole peeled tomatoes, and break them up a bit with a wooden spoon. Cook over medium heat, stirring occasionally, for about 10 minutes. Add salt and pepper to taste.

While the sauce is cooking, coat the bottom of a 13 x 18–inch baking pan with remaining olive oil. Using oiled hands, remove the dough from the bowl carefully. You may be able to stretch it out gently to fit the pan right away, but if not, let dough rest on a floured surface for a few minutes and then fit it into the pan.

Bake the dough for 5 to 7 minutes. Remove from the oven and top with the onion-tomato sauce, American cheese, and shredded white Cheddar and mozzarella cheeses—in that order. Return pan to the oven, reduce the temperature to 400 degrees, and bake until the cheese is bubbly and the crust is golden brown, 10 to 15 minutes.

¼ cup chicken stock or water

¼ cup dried cranberries

2 tablespoons olive oil

1 pound boneless, skinless
chicken breasts

¼ cup chopped fresh sage,
divided

2 teaspoons salt

1 teaspoon freshly ground
black pepper

1 pound orecchiette pasta

2 cups heavy cream

6 ounces fresh goat cheese

Serves 4

Orecchiette Pasta with Grilled Chicken, Cranberries, and Sage Cream

CASBAH, PITTSBURGH
CHEF-OWNER, BIG BURRITO RESTAURANT GROUP, BILL FULLER

Chef Fuller was at the forefront of the food renaissance in Pittsburgh, and this dish hasn't come off the menu in the twenty-two years he's been running Casbah. It's creamy, sweet, and savory all at once—and surprisingly easy to execute.

Bring the stock or water to a boil in a small pot. Add the cranberries and remove from heat. Let stand 20 minutes or so for the cranberries to absorb the liquid.

Lightly oil the chicken breasts. Season with 2 tablespoons of the sage, salt, and pepper. Grill (or cook in a sauté pan or grill pan over medium heat) until no longer pink inside, 10 to 12 minutes, rotating to cook evenly. Let cool, then cut across the grain into slices for four servings and set aside.

Bring 4 quarts of salted water to a boil and cook the pasta according to the package directions. Strain the pasta and reserve.

Place the cream in a wide, shallow sauté pan, bring to a simmer, and reduce by almost half. Add the chicken, cranberries, and remaining 2 tablespoons sage. Return to a simmer. Add the cooked pasta and goat cheese and stir to melt the cheese over low heat. Toss together, adjust seasonings as needed, and serve immediately. If desired, garnish with more fresh sage and a few tablespoons of dried cranberries.

Yeast-raised butter crust

1¾ teaspoons active dry yeast

1½ cups water, lukewarm

3½ cups organic white bread flour

½ teaspoon salt

½ cup (1 stick) butter, cold, chopped

3 large egg yolks

Onion filling

6 tablespoons butter or olive oil

4 cups thinly sliced onions

⅔ cup diced country-style
    slab bacon

Salt and black pepper

4 large eggs

1 cup sour cream or plain yogurt

1 teaspoon caraway seeds

Serves 10 to 16

Pennsylvania Dutch Onion Tart (*Zwiwwelkuche*)

CULINARY HISTORIAN AND COOKBOOK AUTHOR
WILLIAM WOYS WEAVER

In the old days, this tart was a common meal for farmhands on field breaks or any occasion that demanded a quick solution to feeding many mouths at once. Weaver likes this with a glass of Galen Glen's Grüner Veltliner, a dry white wine from an award-winning winery in eastern Pennsylvania. The recipes are adapted from his book Pennsylvania Dutch Country Cooking. Zwiwwelkuche *is the Pennsylvania Dutch equivalent of pizza.*

For the yeast-raised butter crust:
Proof the yeast in the water in a small bowl. In a separate, deep bowl, sift the flour and salt together. Add the butter and rub the mixture through a colander to form fine crumbs, or process in a food processor. Return the crumbs to the bowl and make a well in the center.

Beat the egg yolks into the yeast and pour the mixture into the well in the crumbs. Stir and work into a stiff dough. Knead on a well-floured surface until the dough is soft and spongy and no longer sticks to the fingers, 5 to 10 minutes. Cover and set aside in a warm place to rise until double in bulk, about 1½ hours.

For the onion filling:
While the dough is rising, add the butter or oil to a sauté pan, then the onions. Cover and sweat onions over medium heat until soft, about 5 minutes. Brown the bacon in a separate skillet until golden, then drain off the fat and reserve the bacon.

To assemble:

Preheat the oven to 375 degrees. Press down the dough and roll it ¼ inch thick. Line a shallow baking pan or 14-inch round pizza pan with the dough. Roll the dough edge up to form a rim about 1 inch high. Let the crust rest for about 15 minutes, then spread the sweated onions and cooked bacon evenly over the surface. Sprinkle with salt and pepper to taste.

Beat the eggs until frothy and the color of lemons, then combine with the sour cream or yogurt. Drizzle over the onions and bacon, then scatter caraway seeds over the top. Bake until the egg filling has set and begun to turn golden brown on the surface, 30 to 40 minutes. Serve hot or at room temperature.

Pennsylvania Dutch Steak and Ale Pie

SHAWNEE INN AND GOLF RESORT, SHAWNEE ON DELAWARE
EXECUTIVE CHEF DEAN GARDNER

A hearty meal that makes enough to feed a crowd—or enough to eat one pie now and freeze one for later! This "pie" has no bottom crust.

2 pounds beef top round, cubed

Montreal Steak Seasoning

2 stalks celery, diced large

1 medium Spanish onion, diced large

1 jumbo carrot, diced large

1 garlic clove, finely diced

1 pint Shawnee IPA (or your favorite IPA)

1 beef bouillon cube

2 cups water

1 sprig fresh rosemary

1 sprig fresh thyme

1 bay leaf

2 Yukon Gold potatoes, peeled and diced large

1 (0.87-ounce) packet beef gravy mix

3 tablespoons canola or grape seed oil

2 rolled-out pie crusts, store bought (or see page 116 in Desserts)

1 egg, lightly beaten with 1 tablespoon water or milk

Makes 2 (9-inch) pies

Preheat the oven to 350 degrees.

Season the beef cubes with Montreal Steak Seasoning and sear in a saucepan on high heat until brown on all sides, 3 to 4 minutes. Remove the beef from the saucepan and set aside.

Reduce the heat to medium; add the celery, onion, and carrot and cook until the onion becomes slightly translucent, 3 to 4 minutes. Add the garlic and cook 1 minute more. Add the IPA, bouillon, water, rosemary, thyme, bay leaf, and potatoes. Simmer slowly until the potatoes and vegetables start to soften. Remove the vegetables and potatoes from the saucepan and set aside. Discard the thyme and rosemary stems and the bay leaf.

Follow the gravy mix instructions and use the remaining liquid in the saucepan to yield about 1½ quarts of gravy.

Add the beef, potatoes, and vegetables back into the saucepan, simmer another 15 minutes, and then let cool 10 to 15 minutes.

Transfer the filling to pie plates and top with the crusts. Brush the top of the crusts with the beaten egg. Bake until the pastry turns golden brown, 40 minutes.

Remove from the oven, let stand for 10 minutes, and enjoy!

Pierogi dough

3 to 4 cups flour

¾ cup sour cream, plus more for garnish

5 large eggs, divided

¼ cup finely chopped fresh flat leaf Italian parsley

2 to 3 tablespoons freshly ground black pepper

Yukon potato, onion, and white Cheddar filling

2½ pounds Yukon Gold potatoes, quartered

6 tablespoons butter, divided

1 teaspoon kosher salt

½ teaspoon freshly cracked black pepper

½ cup half-and-half

1 Vidalia onion, diced small

3 cups shredded sharp white Cheddar

Balsamic, wild mushroom, and butternut squash filling

1½ pounds red potatoes, unpeeled, diced small

1 pound butternut squash, diced small

1 cup diced red onion

1 tablespoon granulated garlic (see Note)

Pierogi, Two Ways

29 COOKS, EMMAUS
CHEF-OWNER CINDIE FELDMAN

The Pennsylvania classic gets an upgrade with parsley and black pepper in the dough, along with filling options that include mushrooms, manchego cheese, and butternut squash. The fillings can be made and refrigerated a day or two ahead; just bring them to room temperature before filling the pierogi. Freeze pierogi individually on rimmed baking sheets and then transfer to a zip-top bag. Thaw briefly before cooking.

For the pierogi dough:
In the bowl of a stand mixer fitted with the paddle attachment, combine the flour, sour cream, four eggs, parsley, and pepper until a ball is formed. If it's very sticky, add more flour; if it's dry, add a little more sour cream.

Knead the dough ten to twelve times on a floured surface, then divide into four equal portions. Let rest for 10 minutes, covered loosely with plastic wrap.

For the Yukon potato, onion, and white Cheddar filling:
Place the potatoes in a large pot of water and bring to a boil; cook, uncovered, until fork tender, 20 to 25 minutes.

Put 2 tablespoons of the butter in a large bowl. Drain the potatoes and either rice them on top of the butter or mash them directly into the butter. Add the salt, pepper, and half-and-half. Stir together until well combined; if it's too thick, add more half-and-half.

Sauté the onions in the remaining 4 tablespoons of butter over low heat to caramelize, 15 to 20 minutes. Add to the potato mixture and stir to combine. Refrigerate the potato-onion mixture for about 30 minutes to cool before adding the cheese—otherwise the cheese will get gummy when you cook the pierogi.

(continued on page 104)

2 teaspoons granulated onion
(*see Note*)

½ cup plus 2 tablespoons
olive or avocado oil

2 pounds mixed gourmet
mushrooms, stems removed,
diced medium

3 tablespoons balsamic
reduction glaze

1 tablespoon kosher salt

2 teaspoons freshly ground
black pepper

8 ounces manchego cheese,
shaved or shredded

2 tablespoons butter

2 tablespoons vegetable oil

Makes 40 to 45 large pierogi

For the balsamic, wild mushroom, and butternut squash filling:
Preheat the oven to 400 degrees. In a large bowl, combine the
potatoes, squash, red onion, and granulated garlic and onion
and toss well with ½ cup of the oil.

Roast on a rimmed baking sheet for 10 minutes, then stir the ingredients and bake until softened, another 10 to 15 minutes.

Over medium heat in a large sauté pan, add the remaining 2 tablespoons oil and the roasted vegetables. Toss the ingredients and then
add the mushrooms, stirring to coat. Add the balsamic reduction
glaze, stirring quickly so it does not burn. When the mushrooms are
soft but still have body, remove from heat. Add salt and pepper to
taste. Transfer to paper towels to wick off some of the moisture.

Cool the mixture in the refrigerator for 30 minutes, then stir in the
manchego cheese.

To assemble:
Roll the dough until it is thin but not transparent. Use a biscuit cutter
(2 to 4 inches in diameter) to cut circles from the dough. In a small
bowl, beat the remaining egg. Place 2 to 3 tablespoons of filling in the
center of a circle and brush the perimeter of the dough with the beat–
en egg. Fold the dough over the filling, making a half circle, stretching
slightly until the edges touch. Don't worry if it seems like the pierogi
are too stuffed; the dough will expand when cooked. Press the ends
together lightly and then push your fingers around the filling mound
to get the air out so it doesn't puff up when cooked. Use a fork to
crimp and seal the dough edges. Repeat until all the filling is used.

Boil the pierogi in lightly salted water for 2 to 3 minutes to seal
the edges. Remove them using a slotted spoon to cool on a tray.
You can now cook, refrigerate, or freeze the pierogi.

To cook, in a medium sauté pan over medium heat, heat the butter
with the oil and cook the pierogi until one side is golden brown, 2 to
3 minutes, and then flip to the other side to cook another 2 minutes.
If need be, add a little extra butter.

❧ **Note:** *If you don't have granulated garlic or onion, use half as much of the
powdered form.*

3 cups red wine

3 cups red wine vinegar

10 juniper berries

3 bay leaves

2 whole cloves

3 star anise "blades"

1 teaspoon black peppercorns

1 teaspoon mustard seeds

½ teaspoon cardamom pods

1 teaspoon coriander seeds

3- to 4-pound beef rump, bottom
    round, or chuck roast

Salt and black pepper

2 tablespoons butter

2 tablespoons vegetable oil

1 medium onion, sliced

1 large carrot, cut into
    ½-inch-thick rounds

½ cup flour

2 cups beef stock

1 cup crushed gingersnap cookies

Serves 6 to 8

Sauerbraten

BRAUHAUS SCHMITZ, WURSTHAUS SCHMITZ, AND WHETSTONE
TAVERN, PHILADELPHIA   ❧   EXECUTIVE CHEF JEREMY NOLEN

Sauerbraten is a traditional German roast with an ingenious method for thickening the gravy—crushed gingersnaps. Chef Nolen uses Pennsylvania's own Sweetzel's Spiced Wafers. Serve with potato dumplings and red cabbage or buttered noodles.

Mix the red wine and red wine vinegar in a non-reactive glass or plastic container large enough to hold the beef roast.

In a frying pan over medium heat, toast the juniper berries, bay leaves, cloves, anise, peppercorns, mustard, cardamom, and coriander until fragrant. Stir the toasted spices into the wine and vinegar mix. Place the roast in the marinade, submerging it completely. Use a plate or something heavy to weigh it down. Marinate for at least 3 but preferably 5 days.

Remove the roast and pat dry, reserving the marinade. Season the roast liberally with salt and pepper. Preheat the oven to 350 degrees.

Heat the oil and butter in a large roasting pan on medium-high heat. Add the roast to the pan and sear on all sides until it is a dark brown. Remove the roast and let rest on a plate.

Add the onion and carrots to the roasting pan and cook for about 2 minutes. Add the flour to the pan and stir to incorporate. Whisk in the reserved marinade and beef stock until the flour is incorporated into the liquid. Bring to a boil, add the roast, and cover with a lid (or aluminum foil weighed down by a large lid if you are using a traditional roasting pan).

Roast the sauerbraten until the meat is tender and the internal temperature reaches 175 degrees, 2 to 2½ hours.

Remove the roast from the oven and let rest in the liquid for a few minutes, then remove to a serving platter. Strain the liquid through a fine-mesh strainer into a saucepan.

Add the crushed gingersnaps to the saucepan and simmer until the cookies dissolve and the sauce thickens, 5 to 10 minutes. Taste the gravy and add salt and pepper if desired. Serve immediately.

8 ounces spaghetti or other pasta

3 slices bacon

2 tablespoons olive oil

6 sea scallops

¼ cup chopped red onion

¼ teaspoon minced garlic

Crushed red pepper flakes

½ cup half-and-half

2 tablespoons butter

2 eggs

½ cup grated Pecorino Romano
cheese

2 tablespoons chopped
fresh parsley

Serves 2

Surf and Turf Carbonara for Two

FRANCO'S LOUNGE, RESTAURANT & MUSIC CLUB, WILLIAMSPORT
CHEF-OWNERS MARIA AND FRED DANIELE

The old-school appeal of Franco's cannot be denied—red seats, jazz music, gregarious owners, and downright delicious Italian American fare. They're known for this dish in particular. It serves two but can be easily doubled.

Bring a large pot of salted water to a boil and cook the pasta until tender, according to the package instructions. Drain the pasta and set aside.

Meanwhile, start the bacon in a cold sauté pan and cook over medium-high heat until crisp. Set aside to drain on paper towels.

Add the olive oil and scallops to the pan, still on medium-high heat, cooking a few at a time, being careful not to crowd the pan. Turn them after 2 to 3 minutes—they should be golden brown—and cook another 2 minutes. Remove from the pan and set aside.

Add the onion, garlic, and pepper flakes to taste to the pan. Stir in the half-and-half and butter and bring to a simmer. Add the drained and cooked pasta and stir to combine.

In a small bowl, whisk together the eggs, cheese, and parsley. Add to the sautéed pasta and mix together quickly. Serve immediately.

Zucchini Shepherd's Pie

NORTH COUNTRY BREWING COMPANY, SLIPPERY ROCK
EXECUTIVE CHEF ANDY DAVIN

Chef Davin says this unique meatless take on shepherd's pie is a customer favorite. The zucchini softens when cooked and becomes "mashed." Combined with cheese and bread crumbs, it forms a mouthwatering crispy-creamy top.

Vegetable filling

2 tablespoons olive oil

3 cups finely chopped broccoli

1 cup shredded carrot

1 cup diced tomatoes

½ cup finely diced red onion

2 cups heavy cream

1 cup shredded Cheddar cheese

4 cups cooked rice

1 tablespoon salt

1½ teaspoons black pepper

Zucchini mash

1 large zucchini

3 cups panko bread crumbs

2 cups shredded Asiago cheese

2 tablespoons butter

Salt and black pepper

For the vegetable filling:
Heat a large pan to medium-high heat and add 2 tablespoons olive oil. Add the broccoli, carrot, tomatoes, and red onion and sauté until tender, 5 to 6 minutes.

Add the cream and Cheddar cheese and stir to combine. Add the cooked rice and mix until fully incorporated. Pour into a large (9 x 13-inch or larger) baking dish and let stand. It may look like it won't all fit into the dish, but the rice will absorb the liquid as you make the topping. Preheat the oven to 400 degrees.

For the zucchini mash:
Peel the zucchini and scoop out the seeded center. Chop the zucchini into bite-sized pieces, place in a pot of water, and boil until soft. Drain the zucchini, add the bread crumbs and Asiago cheese, and mix together. Add the butter and stir until it is melted. Lightly seasonwith salt and pepper to taste.

To assemble:
Top the vegetable mixture with the zucchini mash. Bake until golden brown on top, about 45 minutes. Serve hot.

Serves 8 to 10

Desserts & Sweet Treats

Three-Layer Carrot Cake, p. 128

14 ounces Delice De Bourgogne, room temperature

2¾ cups milk

1¼ cups heavy cream

1 vanilla bean, seeded

7 large egg yolks

1 cup sugar

Pinch salt

1 (8-ounce) jar Amarena cherries

Makes 1.5 quarts

Delice De Bourgogne Ice Cream with Amarena Cherries

DI BRUNO BROTHERS, PHILADELPHIA
EXECUTIVE CHEF JAMES LIUZZA

Ice cream made with cheese? You better believe it. Di Bruno Brothers is a well-regarded cheese and gourmet shop in Philadelphia. Thanks to the creamy Delice De Bourgogne cheese, this dessert is tangy and rich— and the imported Amarena cherries, a sour variety preserved in syrup, are worth the splurge.

Remove the rinds of the cheese with a wide, flat knife.

Add the milk, cream, and vanilla bean seeds to a heavy-bottomed saucepan over medium heat. Bring to a low simmer. Keep an eye on it and stir often while you prepare the egg yolks.

Add the egg yolks, sugar, and salt to a large bowl and whisk until light in color, slightly glossy, and fluffy, about 3 minutes. Whisk in the cheese and beat vigorously for another minute or so until it is completely emulsified.

Slowly ladle in a cup of the hot milk mixture into the egg-cheese mixture, whisking constantly. Over low heat, pour the eggs back into the milk and stir until it thickens enough to coat the back of a spoon, 3 to 5 minutes.

Strain the custard through a fine-mesh strainer and cool completely. Refrigerate for at least 2 hours or up to overnight before adding to your ice cream machine. (If you store it overnight, you may need to whisk the mixture again to undo any clumps.)

Follow the manufacturer's instructions for freezing your ice cream, then remove to a separate container and place in the freezer for at least 2 hours, for optimal firmness. Serve topped with Amarena cherries.

Double Chocolate Tahini Cookies

CARRIE HAVRANEK, THE DHARMA KITCHEN

Soom Foods is a tahini brand based in Philadelphia and run by three sisters. This is the most silky and easy-to-work-with tahini, and it's no wonder Chef Michael Solomonov prefers it for his Zahav Brussels Sprouts (see page 47 in Salads & Sides). Soom's chocolate tahini isn't overly sweet, and the sesame seeds add a subtle nutty dimension.

1 cup flour

2 tablespoons flaxseeds

½ teaspoon baking soda

½ teaspoon salt

½ cup (1 stick) butter,
    room temperature

¾ cup sugar

½ cup Soom chocolate tahini

1 large egg

1 cup dark chocolate chips

Makes about 2 dozen cookies

Preheat the oven to 325 degrees.

In a small bowl, whisk together the flour, flaxseeds, baking soda, and salt. Set aside.

In the bowl of a stand mixer fitted with the paddle attachment, cream together the butter, sugar, and tahini at medium speed until lightened in color, 3 to 4 minutes. Add the egg and mix on low to combine, scraping down the sides of the bowl as needed.

With the mixer at low speed, add the flour mixture in three batches. Add the chocolate chips and stir with a wooden spoon to combine.

Drop the dough by tablespoons onto a parchment- or Silpat-lined baking sheet and bake until the cookies start to look crackled, about 10 minutes.

Remove from the oven and let the cookies cool for 5 minutes or so on the baking sheets, then transfer to wire racks to cool completely. Store in an airtight container for up to 4 days.

Pudding

6 tablespoons butter, softened

1 cup plus 2 tablespoons sugar

1½ cups flour

1½ teaspoons baking powder

2 eggs

1½ teaspoons vanilla extract

Dates

1 heaping cup chopped dates

1½ tablespoons flour

1½ teaspoons baking soda

2 cups boiling water

Whipped cream or ice cream,
   for serving (optional)

Makes about 16 individual puddings
or 1 (10-inch) round pudding

English Toffee Pudding

THE SETTLERS INN, HAWLEY   ❧   EXECUTIVE CHEF BEN SUTTER

The Settlers Inn is a historic 1920s-era Arts and Crafts inn nestled in the Pocono Mountains. These "puddings" are little cakes studded with dates, and they're moist but not too sweet. Serve with the caramel sauce from the Stuffed Pumpkin French Toast recipe (see page 13 in Breakfast & Brunch).

For the pudding:
Preheat the oven to 350 degrees.

In the bowl of a stand mixer fitted with the paddle attachment, cream together the butter and sugar on medium speed until lightened in color. Add the flour and baking powder and stir to combine. Add the eggs, one at a time, and the vanilla, and mix well. Scrape down the sides of the bowl if needed.

For the dates:
In a medium bowl, mix together the dates, flour, and baking soda. Pour the boiling water over the dates and stir to quickly mix. Add to the creamed pudding mixture and blend until just mixed. Don't worry if it looks watery.

Divide the batter among sixteen well-greased (or use paper liners) muffin tin cups or a deep 10-inch pie pan. Bake until the puddings are puffed and brown, about 10 minutes. (If using a pie plate, bake about 30 minutes.) Remove from the oven and allow to cool briefly before removing the puddings from the pan. You want them cool enough to handle, but not completely cool.

Serve warm with warm caramel sauce and whipped cream or ice cream. The puddings can be frozen and reheated in the oven at 350 degrees for 10 minutes.

Pie crust

2½ cups flour

¾ teaspoon salt

2 tablespoons sugar

4 tablespoons shortening, frozen

¾ cup (1½ sticks) butter, cold

7 to 8 tablespoons water, ice-cold

Cake batter

6 tablespoons butter

1½ cups sugar

1 tablespoon vanilla extract

2 large eggs

3 cups flour

½ teaspoon salt

1 tablespoon baking powder

1 cup milk

Chocolate sauce

1 cup water, hot

½ cup cocoa powder

1 tablespoon vanilla extract

1½ cups sugar

Makes 2 cakes

Funny Cake

CARRIE HAVRANEK, THE DHARMA KITCHEN

Funny cake is indeed funny. This traditional Pennsylvania Dutch breakfast cake is baked in a pie crust. The chocolate sinks and forms a layer on the bottom. There's nothing funny, however, about the wonderful taste.

For the pie crust:
In a medium bowl, whisk together the flour, salt, and sugar. Cut in the shortening and butter with two forks until the mixture has the consistency of small peas.

Add water 1 tablespoon at a time and mix until the dough comes together but isn't too wet. Cut into two equal dough balls. Roll each into 6-inch-diameter circles and wrap in plastic wrap. Refrigerate for an hour if using immediately or for up to 2 days. Bring the dough to room temperature before using.

For the cake batter:
In the bowl of a stand mixer fitted with the paddle attachment, cream together the butter, sugar, and vanilla. Add the eggs, one at a time, beating at medium speed and scraping down the sides of the bowl as needed.

In a separate bowl, blend the flour, salt, and baking powder. Add the flour mixture and the milk to the creamed butter and sugar, alternating in three separate increments, until just mixed.

For the chocolate sauce:
In a medium bowl, mix together the water, cocoa powder, vanilla, and sugar to form a thin sauce.

To assemble:
Preheat the oven to 375 degrees.

Pour half the cake batter into each of two prepared pie plates. Pour half the chocolate sauce over each cake; it should cover the cake completely. To catch drips, place a large rimmed baking sheet in the oven and set the pie plates on the sheet.

Bake until the cakes are lightly brown around the edges and the top looks swirled with chocolate, 40 to 45 minutes.

Remove from the oven and allow to cool completely before slicing and serving. The cake keeps for about 4 days, covered at room temperature.

❧ **Note**: *This recipe halves well to make just one Funny Cake.*

1 package active dry yeast

¼ cup water, warm

3 eggs

1 cup shortening

4 tablespoons butter

¼ cup whole milk

½ teaspoon salt

3 cups flour, plus more for rolling

2 cups walnuts, chopped

1 cup sugar

1 teaspoon cinnamon

2 large egg whites

Makes 6 or 7 dozen cookies

Kolacky

CARRIE HAVRANEK, THE DHARMA KITCHEN

My mother adapted this recipe from someone on my dad's Hungarian and Austrian side, and she always made it with walnuts. These crescent-shaped cookies are also available in supermarkets, though often spelled and shaped differently, and with apricot, raspberry, or poppy seed filling. It's not uncommon to see them at wedding cookie tables.

In a small bowl, dissolve the yeast in ¼ cup warm water. Separate the eggs, reserve the yolks, and in another small bowl beat the whites until stiff peaks form.

In a large bowl, cream together the shortening and butter. Add the egg yolks, one at a time, followed by the proofed yeast, milk, and salt. Add the 3 cups flour, 1 cup at a time.

Fold in the egg whites with a spatula until incorporated. If the dough sticks to your hands, add more flour; it's okay if the dough feels greasy. Refrigerate overnight.

In a small bowl, combine the walnuts, sugar, and cinnamon. Add the egg whites and stir to combine.

Preheat the oven to 375 degrees.

Take small amounts of dough out of the fridge at a time. On a well-floured surface, roll the dough thin, as for a pie crust. Using a sharp knife, cut the dough into 2½-inch squares. Place about a teaspoon of the walnut filling in the center of each square. Fold up both sets of opposite corners, pinch together, and roll down tightly onto the filling.

Transfer the cookies to an ungreased sheet and bake until they are slightly puffy and golden brown, 10 to 12 minutes.

❧ **Note:** *These cookies keep well for about 5 days in a covered container, or they can be frozen for up to 3 months.*

❧ **Variation—Apricot filling:** *Preheat the oven to 350 degrees. Using store-bought canned filling, spoon about a teaspoon into the center of each square. Pinch opposite corners together and roll down tightly. Bake on ungreased cookie sheets until lightly browned, 10 to 12 minutes.*

Moravian Sugar Cake

RODALE INC., EMMAUS
AUTHOR AND FORMER CEO, MARIA RODALE

The Lehigh Valley area was settled by Moravians in the early 1700s, and they celebrate in church with a "Lovefeast," which is good old-fashioned community building that happens to include sharing cake and coffee right in the pews.

Cake

2 teaspoons active dry yeast

⅓ cup water, lukewarm

½ cup plus ½ teaspoon sugar

½ cup (1 stick) plus 2 tablespoons butter, melted

1 large egg

½ teaspoon salt

1 cup milk, scalded

½ cup mashed potatoes

3 cups flour, plus extra for dusting

Butter to grease pan

Topping

1 cup light brown sugar

½ cup flour

4 tablespoons butter

Pinch cinnamon

Serves 10 to 12

For the cake:
In a small bowl, combine the yeast, water, and the ½ teaspoon sugar and let sit in a warm place until it bubbles, about 10 minutes.

Beat the ½ cup melted butter, egg, salt, and remaining ½ cup sugar until fluffy—it will be thick. Add the scalded milk and mashed potatoes and stir to combine. Stir in the yeast.

Gradually add the flour until the dough starts to come together— it will be sticky. Transfer the dough to a floured surface and knead for about 10 minutes. Place in a greased bowl covered with a clean towel and let rise until the dough doubles, about 2½ hours.

Preheat the oven to 350 degrees.

Grease a 13 x 9-inch pan and press the dough into the pan. Cover and let rest until it puffs up, about 1½ hours.

Brush remaining 2 tablespoons melted butter evenly over the dough, then poke holes in the dough every 2 inches or so with your finger— don't touch the bottom, though.

For the topping:
Combine the sugar, flour, butter, and cinnamon in a bowl to form a crumbly mix. Sprinkle over the dough, making sure to fill the holes.

Bake until golden and cooked through, 20 to 25 minutes. Cut into squares to serve.

✤ **Note:** *This cake is best when eaten within 3 days.*

1 cup (2 sticks) butter, softened

1½ cups peanut butter

1 pound powdered sugar

6 ounces semi-sweet morsels

3 ounces bittersweet morsels

1 teaspoon vanilla extract

2 tablespoons canola oil

Makes about 42 cookies

Peanut Butter Buckeyes

CARRIE HAVRANEK, THE DHARMA KITCHEN

Buckeyes are easy, but they definitely demand attention to detail. Older versions of this recipe called for paraffin wax to keep the buckeyes from going gooey in warm weather. We'll skip the wax and store the completed buckeyes in a cool spot. This recipe is heavily adapted from an online wedding cookie table community.

Combine the butter and peanut butter in the bowl of a stand mixer fitted with the paddle attachment. Cream together briefly to incorporate, just a few seconds. Slowly add the powdered sugar, mixing at low speed. If the mixture is too tacky, add more powdered sugar. If it's too dry, add a little more peanut butter. The dough should be pliable but firm. Cover and refrigerate the dough for 1 hour or up to overnight.

Remove the dough from the fridge. Scoop out a walnut-sized chunk of dough and roll it into a ball. Transfer to a rimmed baking sheet lined with wax paper; repeat with the remaining dough. Cover and refrigerate for 1 hour.

Melt the chocolate chips, vanilla, and oil in a double boiler. Using skewers or toothpicks, dip the peanut butter balls three-quarters of the way into the chocolate, leaving the top exposed to look like a buckeye. Transfer to parchment or wax paper to dry and harden at room temperature (in hot weather, you may need to refrigerate them).

1 ball pie dough for a
   9-inch pie plate

2 cups chopped pecans

1 cup dark corn syrup

1 cup light brown sugar

1 ½ teaspoons salt

1 tablespoon butter

1 teaspoon vanilla extract

3 eggs

Serves 8

Pecan Pie

MARSHA BROWN, NEW HOPE
OWNER'S MOTHER OPHELIA BROWN

Situated in an old church, Marsha Brown is an upscale Southern restaurant, and this pecan pie is a well-known menu staple. Use your favorite pie crust, or halve the amounts for the crust in the Funny Cake recipe (see page 116 in this chapter). This recipe comes from Marsha's mother, Ophelia.

Preheat the oven to 350 degrees.

Roll out the pie dough on a floured surface to about 12 inches in diameter. Carefully transfer the dough to a 9-inch pie plate, pressing the dough gently into the plate so there are no bubbles. Press the edges into place around the perimeter of the plate and trim any excess around the rim.

Roughly chop the pecans by hand or in a food processor and place them into the prepared pie shell.

Combine the corn syrup, brown sugar, salt, butter, and vanilla in the bowl of a stand mixer fitted with the paddle attachment and mix on low speed.

In a separate bowl, beat the eggs lightly and then gradually add them to the syrup mixture, mixing on low speed to combine. Pour the mixture into the pie shell, filling to just below the beginning of the pie crust edge.

Bake in the oven for 45 to 50 minutes—the top will look nicely crackled—then remove from the oven to cool completely. Serve with vanilla ice cream or a dollop of whipped cream.

⊱ *Note: Pecan pie keeps for at least a week, covered, in the refrigerator.*

8 ounces almond paste

½ cup granulated sugar

½ cup powdered sugar,
    firmly packed

2 large egg whites

½ teaspoon vanilla extract

3 tablespoons flour

Pinch salt

1 cup pine nuts

Makes about 30 cookies

Pignoli

MARIE VOKISH, PITTSBURGH   ⁚   HOME-BASED PASTRY CHEF

Pignoli are classic almond and pine nut cookies that get their lift and crackle from almond paste and egg whites. They're easy to make and part of a classic wedding table spread. Pine nuts can be pricey, but they make the cookie special. Vokish is known to make hundreds of these for weddings.

Combine the almond paste and the sugars in the bowl of a stand mixer fitted with the paddle attachment. Beat on low speed until the mixture is the texture of small crumbs.

Add the egg whites and vanilla. Beat on high, scraping the sides of the bowl, until dough forms a smooth paste, about 3 minutes. Add the flour and salt, and mix until just combined. Cover and refrigerate for 1 hour.

Preheat the oven to 325 degrees. Line two cookie sheets with parchment paper.

Put the pine nuts in a small, shallow bowl. Using slightly dampened fingers, drop the batter 1 teaspoon at a time into the nuts, then quickly flip the dough balls onto a cookie sheet so the nut-free side is face down.

Bake until lightly golden, 14 to 16 minutes. Gently slide the parchment paper off the baking sheets onto a wire rack. When the cookies are completely cool, peel gently from the parchment. Store cookies in an airtight container between wax paper.

Pumpkin Whoopie Pies

FLYING MONKEY BAKERY, PHILADELPHIA
PASTRY CHEF-OWNER ELIZABETH HALEN

Patrons arrive early at Flying Monkey in Reading Terminal Market because these whoopies fly outta there. Change the filling by adding toasted nuts, chocolate chips, or maple syrup.

Cookies

4 cups flour

1 tablespoon plus
   1 teaspoon cinnamon

2 teaspoons ground ginger

1 teaspoon salt

1 teaspoon baking powder

1 teaspoon baking soda

¾ cup buttermilk

1 cup vegetable oil

2 cups sugar

2 large eggs

½ teaspoon vanilla extract

2 cups pumpkin puree

Cream cheese fluff filling

4 tablespoons butter, softened

8 ounces cream cheese, softened

3 to 4 cups powdered sugar, sifted

¾ cup marshmallow fluff

1 teaspoon vanilla extract

Makes 12 whoopie pies

For the cookies:
Preheat the oven to 350 degrees. Line a baking sheet with parchment paper.

In a large bowl, sift together the flour, cinnamon, ginger, salt, baking powder, and baking soda.

In a separate bowl, whisk together the buttermilk, oil, sugar, eggs, and vanilla. Add the pumpkin and stir to combine. Pour the wet mixture into the dry and mix with a spatula until combined.

Use a ¼-cup cookie scoop to drop the batter onto the baking sheet. Bake until the cookies spring back from your touch, 12 to 14 minutes, rotating the trays halfway through the baking process.

Transfer to a wire rack to cool completely before filling.

For the cream cheese fluff filling:
Cream together the butter and cream cheese in a stand mixer fitted with the paddle attachment at medium speed until combined, 2 to 3 minutes. Slowly add the sugar, marshmallow fluff, and vanilla.

To assemble:
Spoon a dollop of filling onto the flat side of one cookie and make a sandwich by placing another cookie on top.

Scholl Orchard Apple Crumble

SCHOLL ORCHARDS, KEMPTON   ❧   OWNER JUNE SCHOLL

The Scholl family are third-generation farmers, with more than forty acres and a dizzying number of apple types—and some delicious peaches, too. This apple crumble is a recipe from family matriarch June Scholl, adapted slightly by adding a little more butter and mixing together brown and granulated sugars to deepen and sweeten the taste. Buy the best apples you can possibly find—it will make all the difference. I used a combination of Honeycrisp and Fuji.

4 to 5 cups firm apples,
   peeled and thinly sliced

1 teaspoon cinnamon

¼ cup water

¾ cup flour

⅓ cup granulated sugar

⅓ cup brown sugar

6 tablespoons butter, cold, cubed

Serves 6 to 8

Preheat the oven to 350 degrees.

In a medium bowl, combine the peeled apples with the cinnamon and water. Set aside.

In a second medium bowl, combine the flour, sugars, and butter, working the butter between your fingers until the mixture forms pea-size crumbs.

Pour the apple filling into an 8 x 8-inch baking dish and then sprinkle the crumb topping to completely cover the filling. Bake until bubbling and lightly browned, about 45 minutes.

Remove from the oven to cool completely. Serve warm with vanilla ice cream.

❧ **Note:** *The crumble will keep in the refrigerator, covered, for up to 5 days.*

2 balls pie dough for
    9-inch pie plate

1 cup molasses

½ cup brown sugar

2 eggs, beaten

1 teaspoon baking soda

1 cup water, hot

2 cups flour

¾ cup brown sugar

½ teaspoon cinnamon

⅔ cup shortening or butter,
    cold, cubed

Makes 2 (9-inch) pies

Shoofly Pie

BIRD-IN-HAND BAKE SHOP, BIRD-IN-HAND
CEO JOHN SMUCKER AND GRANDMA SMUCKER

When you think of Pennsylvania, you think of this sweet pie, full of molasses and brown sugar; it actually descends from a cake made at the U.S. centennial in Philadelphia in 1876. The Smucker family sells Shoofly Pie at their Bird-in-Hand Bakery. The recipe makes two pies—you never know when company might show up, or you can freeze the second one. Use the pie crust recipe for Funny Cake (see page 116 in this chapter).

Preheat the oven to 400 degrees.

Roll out the pie crust on a floured surface to about 12 inches in diameter. Carefully transfer the dough to a 9-inch pie plate, pressing the dough gently into the plate so there are no bubbles. Press the edges into place around the perimeter of the plate and trim any excess around the rim. Repeat with the second pie plate.

Mix the molasses, brown sugar, and eggs in a bowl with a whisk or in the bowl of a stand mixer fitted with the paddle attachment.

Dissolve the baking soda in hot water and add to the sugary egg mixture. Stir to combine. Carefully pour into the pie shells, going to about ½ inch from the top edge.

In a medium bowl, mix the flour, brown sugar, cinnamon, and shortening or butter until it forms a coarse meal. Sprinkle over the top of the pies, forming a slight mound in the center.

Bake for 10 minutes, then reduce the temperature to 350 degrees and bake another 50 minutes. The crust should be golden brown, and a toothpick inserted in the center of the pies will come out clean. Serve immediately with a dollop of whipped cream or vanilla ice cream.

❧ *Note: Shoofly Pie will store at room temperature for up to 3 days.*

Carrot cake

3 pounds carrots

2 cups golden raisins

2 cups chopped pecans

3 cups vegetable oil

8 large eggs

4 cups flour

4 cups sugar

4 teaspoons baking soda

4 teaspoons cinnamon

2 teaspoons salt

Cinnamon cream cheese frosting

4 pounds cream cheese,
    room temperature

1 cup (2 sticks) butter,
    room temperature

1½ pounds powdered sugar

4 teaspoons cinnamon

1 teaspoon vanilla extract

Serves 10 to 12

Three-Layer Carrot Cake

TOP CUT STEAK HOUSE, CENTER VALLEY
CORPORATE CHEF, PAXOS RESTAURANTS, CHRISTOPHER HEATH

This decadent cake, which keeps for days, is often requested for special occasions at Top Cut. The chef developed it based on his wife's grandmother's recipe. Garnish with chopped nuts, caramel sauce, or whatever you like. This is a celebratory cake—if you don't have 10-inch pans or don't want to make something so large, the recipe can be halved and baked in two eight-inch round cake pans.

For the carrot cake:
Preheat the oven to 325 degrees.

Blend the carrots in a food processor until well shredded. Mix the raisins and pecans together in a separate bowl.

In the bowl of a stand mixer with the paddle attachment, combine the carrots, oil, and eggs and mix for 2 minutes. In a large bowl, blend together the flour, sugar, baking soda, cinnamon, and salt. Slowly add the dry ingredients to the carrot mixture and mix well on low speed. Add the pecans and raisins.

Spray three 10-inch cake pans with cooking oil and line with parchment paper. Divide the batter evenly among the pans and bake until a toothpick inserted in the middle comes out clean and the cakes pull away from the sides of the pans, 45 to 50 minutes. Remove from the oven and cool in the pans for half an hour, then turn the cakes out onto wire racks to cool completely.

For the cinnamon cream cheese frosting:
In the bowl of a stand mixer fitted with the paddle attachment, cream together the cream cheese and butter on medium speed until smooth, 2 to 3 minutes. Add the powdered sugar, cinnamon, and vanilla and mix to combine.

To assemble:

When the cakes have cooled, place one cake as the bottom layer on a platter and spread about 1 cup frosting over the top with a spatula. Repeat with each layer and then frost all around the outside of the cake. Using the remaining frosting, create decorative swirls over the sides and top of the cake.

This cake can be prepared a day or two in advance. Cover with a cake dome and refrigerate, then serve either cold or at room temperature.

✎ **Note:** *You can garnish the cake with chopped nuts, caramel sauce (see the Stuffed Pumpkin French Toast recipe on page 13 in Breakfast & Brunch), or piped icing on top. With this recipe as a guideline, make the cake your own. Toast the pecans or substitute walnuts. Add dried cranberries along with the raisins for a sweet-tart element. You can also slow-roast extra carrots with a touch of sugar and honey, puree, and then strain excess water in a fine-mesh sieve over a bowl. Add the puree to the cinnamon cream cheese frosting to intensify the carrot taste. Or replace the cinnamon with nutmeg or allspice.*

3½ cups whole milk

1½ cups sweetened condensed milk
    (Eagle Brand preferred)

½ cup sugar

2⅔ cups heavy whipping cream

2 tablespoons vanilla extract

Makes ½ gallon

Vanilla Ice Cream

PENN STATE BERKEY CREAMERY, STATE COLLEGE, UNIVERSITY PARK

This recipe is the base for ice creams served at Penn State University's historic creamery, which dates to 1889. People line up for their favorites, and professionals come here for ice cream training. If you have a standard ice cream maker, this recipe works best if you freeze it in two batches (the recipe yields a half gallon), or you could cut the recipe in half.

Pour the whole milk into a large bowl and stir in the sweetened condensed milk. Add the sugar and stir to dissolve. Add the whipping cream and vanilla and stir until thoroughly blended. Chill in the refrigerator, covered, for at least an hour or up to overnight.

Freeze and churn according to the manufacturer's instructions for your machine. For a hand-cranked ice cream maker, place the dasher in the canister and fill about three-quarters full with batter. Place the canister in the bucket and surround with ice and liberal amounts of rock salt. Crank continuously until the ice cream thickens and the handle becomes hard to turn, adding ice and salt as needed. Pull the canister from the bucket, remove the dasher and scrape it clean, and enjoy the fruits of your labor!

❧ **Note:** *For variety, you can add up to ¾ cup diced fruit, up to ¼ cup syrup of your choice (such as chocolate fudge), or up to ½ cup chopped nuts.*

Cook's Pantry

Chow Krout, p. 134

1 pound red beets

½ bunch fresh dill

1 garlic clove

1 teaspoon kosher salt

14 cups filtered water

1 dozen eggs

Makes 1 dozen eggs

Beet (Kvass) Pickled Eggs

PHICKLE.COM, PHILADELPHIA ❧ COOKBOOK AUTHOR, BLOGGER, AND FERMENTATION EDUCATOR AMANDA FEIFER

Beet pickled eggs are a PA Dutch staple. This recipe goes in two phases— first you make the kvass, then you pickle eggs in it.

Remove the tops and tails from the beets. Remove any pits or soft parts on the peel, but leave the peels otherwise intact. Cut the beets into eighths, making pieces no smaller than 1 x 1 inch and no larger than 2 x 2 inches.

Place the dill, garlic, and salt in a gallon jar (or two 1-quart jars) and cover with the beet pieces. Add the water and shake the jar a bit to dissolve the salt.

Cover the jar medium tight, allowing room for carbon dioxide to escape, but preventing air from getting in. Leave to ferment at room temperature for 10 days to 2 weeks, gently shaking the jar each day to disturb the surface and prevent yeasts from forming. The longer it sits, the more sour it will taste. When fermented to your liking, use a fine-mesh strainer to pour off the liquid—that's the kvass.

When the kvass is ready, bring a pot of water to a boil. Add a dozen eggs in their shells. Set the timer for 9 minutes and then stir the eggs gently for the first minute.

Add ice to a medium bowl with a bit of cold water. When the eggs are finished, transfer to the ice bath to fully cool.

Once cool, peel the eggs and place them in a ½-gallon lidded jar. Pour the finished kvass into the jar until the eggs are just covered. Refrigerate for 3 days, or up to 2 weeks if you like a more sour kvass. Remove the eggs as desired for eating, always using clean implements.

Carolina mustard sauce

¼ cup cider vinegar

¼ cup plus 1 ½ tablespoons
   brown sugar

¼ cup honey

¼ cup molasses

1 ½ teaspoons chipotle sauce

1 ½ teaspoons Worcestershire sauce

2 tablespoons ketchup

¼ teaspoon black pepper

1 cup yellow mustard

Makes about 2 cups

St. Louis barbecue sauce

1 cup brown sugar

½ cup red wine vinegar

½ cup water

1 ¼ cups ketchup

2 tablespoons barbecue sauce

4 teaspoons Worcestershire sauce

2 teaspoons smoked paprika

2 teaspoons black pepper

1 ½ teaspoons ground mustard

½ teaspoon kosher salt

½ teaspoon cayenne pepper

Makes about 3 cups

Carolina Mustard Sauce and St. Louis Barbecue Sauce

IRON HILL BREWERY, PHILADELPHIA   ∾   CO-FOUNDER AND DIRECTOR OF CULINARY OPERATIONS KEVIN DAVIES

Either of these barbecue sauces goes well with Iron Hill's Braised Pulled Pork Sandwich (see page 52 in Sandwiches).

For Carolina mustard sauce:
In a large mixing bowl, add the vinegar, brown sugar, honey, molasses, chipotle sauce, Worcestershire sauce, ketchup, black pepper, and mustard. Whisk thoroughly to combine. Transfer to a covered container and refrigerate for up to 2 weeks.

For St. Louis barbecue sauce:
In a large mixing bowl, vigorously whisk together the brown sugar, vinegar, and water for 20 seconds. Add the ketchup, barbecue sauce, Worcestershire sauce, paprika, black pepper, ground mustard, salt, and cayenne pepper. Whisk to combine, transfer to a covered container, and refrigerate for up to 7 days.

¾ pound green cabbage

¼ pound red cabbage

4 teaspoons kosher salt

½ cup snow peas,
    ends and strings removed

1 large carrot

½ small head broccoli

½ small onion, diced
    (about ½ cup)

1-inch-square piece fresh horseradish,
    finely grated

⅛ teaspoon ground allspice

⅛ teaspoon ground cardamom

⅛ teaspoon black pepper

Makes 1 quart

Chow Kraut

PHICKLE.COM, PHILADELPHIA ❧ COOKBOOK AUTHOR,
BLOGGER, AND FERMENTATION EDUCATOR AMANDA FEIFER

*Chow chow is a classic pickled vegetable mix common on Pennsylvania
tables; it's a way to preserve late summer produce. This one takes its cue
from sauerkraut and changes colors as it ferments. Make sure you start
with clean hands and a sterilized glass jar with a lid.*

Remove the outer leaves (reserving one for packing) and slice the
cabbages into uniform pieces. In a large bowl, combine the cabbage
and salt. Chop the snow peas and carrot crosswise into ½-inch pieces
and add to the cabbage. Break the broccoli into the smallest possible
florets, discarding the large stem. Slice smaller stem bits into small
pieces and add the florets and stem pieces (about 2 cups total) to the
bowl. Next add the diced onion and grated horseradish and toss with
your hands. Let the kraut sit for 30 minutes and then add the allspice,
cardamom, and black pepper, tossing to distribute.

Pack the kraut mixture into a sterilized 1-quart glass jar. It will look
like it won't fit, but it will. Keep pressing it down, using a cabbage
leaf to remove air bubbles and pack it more tightly. Once it's all in
the jar, top with the cabbage leaf. Cap tightly and ferment at room
temperature for 7 to 10 days.

Stored in the refrigerator, this chow kraut keeps indefinitely.

(see photograph on page 131)

2 cups (4 sticks) butter, softened

2 tablespoons Hershey's
   chocolate syrup

1 tablespoon Hershey's
   cocoa powder

Makes 32 servings

Hershey's Chocolate Butter

HERSHEY HOTELS AND RESORTS, HERSHEY
EXECUTIVE PASTRY CHEF CHER HARRIS

*This recipe couldn't be simpler, but it really does make whatever you're
eating a little sweeter and more special. The Hershey Resorts serves this
with white and multigrain breads. Feel free to add it to toast, bagels,
muffins, pancakes—anywhere you'd use butter and a hit of chocolate
would make sense.*

In the bowl of a stand mixer with the paddle attachment, combine
the softened butter, chocolate syrup, and cocoa powder. Whip until
smooth. Store in a lidded container or jar for up to 2 weeks in the
refrigerator and 1 month in the freezer.

1 (4-pound) pumpkin or butternut or longneck squash

1 teaspoon cinnamon

½ teaspoon freshly grated nutmeg

½ teaspoon ground ginger

¼ teaspoon ground allspice

¼ teaspoon ground cloves

2 teaspoons apple cider vinegar

½ cup maple syrup

Makes 1½ pints

Maple-Sweetened Pumpkin Butter

FOOD IN JARS BLOGGER AND COOKBOOK AUTHOR MARISA MCCLELLAN, PHILADELPHIA

Delicious on toast, stirred into oatmeal, or right out of the jar, pumpkin butter is a seasonal specialty with a short shelf life—it cannot be canned by traditional means because it is low in acid and very dense. Look for pumpkins with lots of warts on the outside; it's a sign of sweetness.

Preheat the oven to 350 degrees. Cover a baking sheet with foil. Prick the top of the pumpkin with the tip of a knife three or four times. Roast the pumpkin until it slumps slightly and yields to the tines of a fork, about 45 minutes.

Cool the pumpkin to room temperature, which may take an hour. Cut in half, pull away the seeds and strings, and use a spoon to scrape the flesh from the skin. Put the flesh into a blender or food processor and blend until smooth. A 4-pound pumpkin should yield 5 to 6 cups of puree.

Pour the puree into a 12-inch skillet and heat over medium-low. Stir regularly until all the water has been cooked out—which may take 20 minutes, depending on your pumpkin. Stir in the cinnamon, nutmeg, ginger, allspice, and cloves, and then the apple cider vinegar and maple syrup.

The pumpkin butter is ready when it sits high in the bowl of a spoon. Funnel the finished butter into lidded refrigerator- or freezer-safe containers. It will keep 2 to 3 weeks in the refrigerator and up to a year in the freezer.

Tomato, onion, and golden raisin chutney

3 tablespoons olive oil

2 medium onions, finely diced (about 2 cups)

¾ teaspoon salt

¼ teaspoon black pepper

⅓ cup golden raisins

1½ tablespoons brown sugar

¼ teaspoon ground cardamom

1 to 2 tablespoons red wine or sherry

1 (15-ounce) can fire-roasted diced tomatoes

½ Thai chile pepper or a pinch chile flakes

Makes about 12 ounces

Cilantro coconut chutney

1 small green chile

1 pinch ground cumin

1 tablespoon agave nectar

1 large bunch fresh cilantro, tough ends removed

1 lime, zested and juiced

2 cups unsweetened flaked coconut

Salt and black pepper

1 to 2 tablespoons extra virgin olive oil, as needed

Makes 1 pint

Tomato, Onion, and Golden Raisin Chutney and Cilantro Coconut Chutney

CAFÉ SANTOSHA, TREXLERTOWN 🙰 OWNER SARAH COLLINS

These two chutney recipes accompany the Indian Breakfast Bowl (see page 10 in Breakfast & Brunch). They're equally tasty on toast or in a sandwich.

For the tomato, onion, and golden raisin chutney:
Heat the olive oil in a medium sauté pan and sauté the onions, stirring occasionally, until they turn golden brown, 5 to 8 minutes. Add the salt and pepper and sauté a few minutes more. Add the raisins, sugar, and cardamom and stir to combine.

Deglaze with wine or sherry and scrape any bits that are sticking to the pan. Add the tomatoes and chile pepper. Simmer and cook uncovered, stirring occasionally, for 20 minutes. Refrigerated, the chutney will keep for about 2 weeks. Serve at room temperature.

For the cilantro coconut chutney:
In the bowl of a food processor, pulse together the chile, cumin, agave nectar, cilantro, lime zest and juice, flaked coconut, and salt and pepper to taste. Add the oil while the machine is running. The chutney should be a thick paste, not thin like pesto. Taste and adjust seasoning as needed. Serve at room temperature.

sources for specialty ingredients and other products

Acquerello Carnaroli rice: Gustiamo, gustiamo.com

Espelette pepper: Sur la Table, surlatable.com

Fennel pollen, granulated garlic and granulated onion:
    The Spice House, thespicehouse.com

Frantoia Extra Virgin Olive Oil: Williams–Sonoma, williams–sonoma.com
    or amazon.com

Maine Coast Sea Vegetables: kombu, seaweed; seaveg.com

Penzeys Spices: black or brown mustard seeds, za'atar; penzeys.com

Soom Tahini: soomfoods.com

Sun Noodle: ramen; sunnoodle.com

Tovolo King Cube Ice Trays: tovolo.com or amazon.com

Wigle Whiskey: wiglewhiskey.com

contributors

3rd & Ferry Fish Market
56 South 3rd Street
Easton, PA 18042
(610) 829-1404
thirdandferry.com

29 Cooks
4030 Chestnut Street
Emmaus, PA 18049
(484) 951-0442
29cooks.com

Alison Conklin
Emmaus, PA
alisonconklin.com

Amanda Feifer
phickle.com

Apollo Grill
85 West Broad Street
Bethlehem, PA 18018
(610) 865-9600
apollogrill.com

Apteka
4606 Penn Avenue
Pittsburgh, PA 15224
aptekapgh.com

Barrel 21 Distillery & Dining
2225 North Atherton Street
State College, PA 16803
(814) 308-9522
barrel21distillery.com

Bill Sell's Bold
1413 11th Avenue
Altoona, PA 16601
(814) 946-0301
billsellsbold.com

Bird-in-Hand Bake Shop
542 Gibbons Road
Bird-in-Hand, PA 17505
(717) 656-7947
bihbakeshop.com

The Blind Pig Kitchen
236 Iron Street
Bloomsburg, PA 17815
(570) 784-2656
blindpigkitchen.com

Bolete
1740 Seidersville Road
Bethlehem, PA 18015
(610) 868-6505
boleterestaurant.com

Brauhaus Schmitz
718 South Street
Philadelphia, PA 19147
(267) 909-8814
brauhausschmitz.com

Breakaway Farms
2446 Valley View Road
Mount Joy, PA 17552
(717) 653-2470
breakawayfarms.net

Butcher and the Rye
212 Sixth Street
Pittsburgh, PA 15222
(412) 391-2752
butcherandtherye.com

Café Santosha
7150 Hamilton Boulevard
Trexlertown, PA 18087
(610) 366-1711
healthyalt.com

Casbah
229 South Highland Avenue
Pittsburgh, PA 15206
(412) 661-5656
casbahpgh.com

The Circular at the Hotel Hershey
100 Hotel Road
Hershey, PA 17033
(844) 330-1711
thehotelhershey.com

The Colony Meadery
905 Harrison Street
Allentown, PA 18103
(855) 632-3669
colonymeadery.com

Cooper's Seafood House
701 North Washington Avenue
Scranton, PA 18509
(570) 346-6883
coopers-seafood.com

Dad's Hat
925 Canal Street
Bristol, PA 19007
(215) 781-8300
dadshatrye.com

Di Bruno Brothers
1730 Chestnut Street
Philadelphia, PA 19103
(215) 665-9200
dibruno.com

Dundore & Heister
1331 Penn Avenue
Wyomissing, PA 19610
(610) 374-6328
dundoreandheister.com

Flying Monkey Bakery
Reading Terminal Market
1146 Arch Street, #431
Philadelphia, PA 19107
(215) 928-0340
flyingmonkeyphilly.com

Forksville General Store
& Restaurant
22 Bridge Street
Forksville, PA 18616
(570) 924-4982
forksvillestore.com

Franco's Lounge,
Restaurant & Music Club
12 West Fourth Street
Williamsport, PA 17770
(570) 327-1840
francoslounge.com

High Street on Market
308 Market Street
Philadelphia, PA 19106
(215) 625-0988
highstreetonmarket.com

The Historic Fairfield Inn
15 West Main Street
Fairfield, PA 17320
(717) 642-5410
thefairfieldinn.com

The Hotel Hershey
100 Hotel Road
Hershey, PA 17033
(717) 533-2171
thehotelhershey.com

Iron Hill Brewery
3 West Gay Street
West Chester, PA 19380
(610) 738-9600
ironhillbrewery.com

JoBoy's Brew Pub
27-31 East Main Street
Lititz, PA 17543
(717) 568-8330
joboysbrewpub.com

Joe's Steaks + Soda Shop
6030 Torresdale Avenue
Philadelphia, PA 19135
(215) 535-9405
joessteaks.com

John J. Jeffries Restaurant
300 Harrisburg Avenue
Lancaster, PA 17603
(717) 431-3307
johnjjeffries.com

Kathy's Café
21 South Main Street
Hughesville, PA 17737
(570) 584-5356

A Kilt and a Cuppa
1536 Seidersville Road
Bethlehem, PA 18015
(484) 456-9238
akiltandacuppa.com

The Kind Café
16 North Market Street
Selinsgrove, PA 17870
(570) 374-0663
thekindcafe.com

Laurel Highlands Meadery
106 4th Street
Irwin, PA 15642
(724) 249-6323
laurelhighlandsmeadery.com

Lew Bryson
Twitter: @lewbryson

The Lodge at Woodloch
109 River Birch Lane
Hawley, PA 18428
(570) 685-8500
thelodgeatwoodloch.com

Ma(i)son
230 North Prince Street
Lancaster, PA 17603
(717) 293-5060
maisonlancaster.com

Marisa McClellan
foodinjars.com

Marsha Brown
15 South Main Street
New Hope, PA 18938
(215) 862-7044
marshabrownrestaurant.com

The Mint Gastropub
1223 West Broad Street
Bethlehem, PA 18018
(610) 419-3810
bethlehemmint.com

Mister Lee's Noodles
Easton Public Market
325 Northampton Street
Easton, PA 18042
(610) 829-2799
misterleesnoodles.com

Molinari's
322 East Third Street
Bethlehem, PA 18015
(610) 625-9222
molinarimangia.com

North Country Brewing Company
141 South Main Street
Slippery Rock, PA 16057
(724) 794-2337
northcountrybrewing.com

Note Bistro & Wine Bar
1530 North 2nd Street
Harrisburg, PA 17102
(717) 412-7415
notewinebar.com

Old Tioga Farm
1432 Old Tioga Turnpike
Stillwater, PA 17878
(570) 855-8108
oldtiogafarm.com

Penn State Berkey Creamery
119 Rodney A. Erickson
Food Science Building
University Park, PA 16802
(814) 863-7535
creamery.psu.edu

Picasso's
Millcreek Mall Complex
2060 Interchange Road
Erie, PA 16565
(814) 866-1183
picassoserie.com

Portabello's
115 West State Street
Kennett Square, PA 19348
(610) 925-4984
portabellosofkennettsquare.com

Rachel's Café & Creperie
201 West Walnut Street
Lancaster, PA 17603
(717) 399-3515
rachelscreperie.com

Ralph's Italian Restaurant
760 South 9th Street
Philadelphia, PA 19147
(215) 627-6011
ralphsrestaurant.com

Revival Kitchen
64 South Main Street
Reedsville, PA 17084
(717) 667-7089
revivalkitchen.com

Maria Rodale
@mariarodale
(Twitter and Instagram)

Savory Grille
2934 Seisholtzville Road
Macungie, PA 18062
(610) 845-2010
savorygrille.com

Scholl Orchards
3057 Center Street
Bethlehem, PA 18107
schollorchards.com

The Settlers Inn
4 Main Avenue
Hawley, PA 18428
(570) 226-2993
thesettlersinn.com

Shawnee Inn and Golf Resort
100 Shawnee Inn Drive
Shawnee on Delaware, PA 18356
(570) 424-4000
shawneeinn.com

Social Still Distillery
530 East 3rd Street
Bethlehem, PA 18015
(610) 625-4585
socialstill.com

Soom Foods
428 East Erie Avenue
Philadelphia, PA 19134
(267) 457-3613
soomfoods.com

The Sticky Elbow
631 Washington Boulevard
Williamsport, PA 17701
(570) 323-8888
thestickyelbow.com

Talula's Table
102 West State Street
Kennett Square, PA 19348
(610) 444-8255
talulastable.com

Tessaro's
4601 Liberty Avenue
Pittsburgh, PA 15224
(412) 682-6809
tessaros.com

Top Cut Steak House
The Promenade Shops
at Saucon Valley
2880 Center Valley Parkway, #625
Center Valley, PA 18034
(610) 841-7100
topcutsteak.com

Trenthouse Inn Bed and Breakfast
2008 Copper Kettle Highway
Rockwood, PA 15557
(814) 353-8222
trenthouseinn.net

Tria Café
123 South 18th Street
Philadelphia, PA 19103
(215) 972-8742
triaphilly.com

Two Rivers Brewing Company
542 Northampton Street
Easton, PA 18042
(610) 829-1131
tworiversbrewing.com

Vernick Food & Drink
2031 Walnut Street
Philadelphia, PA 19103
(267) 639-6644
vernickphilly.com

Vetri Cucina
1312 Spruce Street
Philadelphia, PA 19107
(215) 732-3478
vetricucina.com

Victory Brewing Company
420 Acorn Lane
Downingtown, PA 19335
(610) 873-0881
victorybeer.com

Voodoo Brewery
215 Arch Street
Meadville, PA 16335
(814) 337-3676
voodoobrewery.com

Weyerbacher Brewing Company
905 Line Street
Easton, PA 18042
(610) 559-5561
weyerbacher.com

Whitfield at Ace Hotel
120 South Whitfield Street
Pittsburgh, PA 15206
(412) 626-3090
whitfieldpgh.com

Wigle Whiskey Distillery
2401 Smallman Street
Pittsburgh, PA 15222
(412) 224-2827
wiglewhiskey.com

William Woys Weaver, PhD
Keystone Center for the Study of
Regional Foods and Food Tourism
P.O. Box 75
Devon, PA 19333
williamwoysweaver.com
keystonekitchen.org

Zahav
237 St. James Place
Philadelphia, PA 19106
(215) 625-8800
zahavrestaurant.com

index

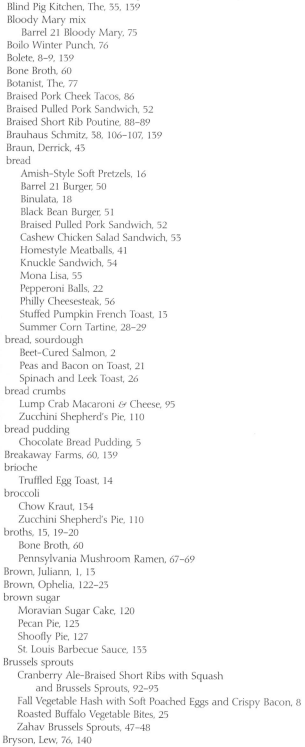

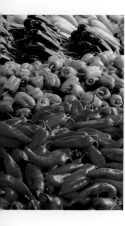